CW00551871

FRENCH
VOCABULARY

ENGLISH-FRENCH

The most useful words
To expand your lexicon and sharpen
your language skills

3000 words

French vocabulary for English speakers - 3000 words

By Andrey Taranov

T&P Books vocabularies are intended for helping you learn, memorize, and revise foreign words. The dictionary is divided into themes, covering all major spheres of everyday activities, business, science, culture, etc.

The process of learning words using T&P Books' theme-based dictionaries gives you the following advantages:

- Correctly grouped source information predetermines success at subsequent stages of word memorization
- Availability of words derived from the same root allowing memorization of word units (rather than separate words)
- Small units of words facilitate the process of establishing associative links needed for consolidation of vocabulary
- Level of language knowledge can be estimated by the number of learned words

T&P Books Publishing
www.tpbooks.com

ISBN: 978-1-78071-009-9

FRENCH VOCABULARY
for English speakers

T&P Books vocabularies are intended to help you learn, memorize, and review foreign words. The vocabulary contains over 3000 commonly used words arranged thematically.

- Vocabulary contains the most commonly used words
- Recommended as an addition to any language course
- Meets the needs of beginners and advanced learners of foreign languages
- Convenient for daily use, revision sessions, and self-testing activities
- Allows you to assess your vocabulary

Special features of the vocabulary

- Words are organized according to their meaning, not alphabetically
- Words are presented in three columns to facilitate the reviewing and self-testing processes
- Words in groups are divided into small blocks to facilitate the learning process
- The vocabulary offers a convenient and simple transcription of each foreign word

The vocabulary has 101 topics including:

Basic Concepts, Numbers, Colors, Months, Seasons, Units of Measurement, Clothing & Accessories, Food & Nutrition, Restaurant, Family Members, Relatives, Character, Feelings, Emotions, Diseases, City, Town, Sightseeing, Shopping, Money, House, Home, Office, Working in the Office, Import & Export, Marketing, Job Search, Sports, Education, Computer, Internet, Tools, Nature, Countries, Nationalities and more ...

T&P BOOKS' THEME-BASED DICTIONARIES

The Correct System for Memorizing Foreign Words

Acquiring vocabulary is one of the most important elements of learning a foreign language, because words allow us to express our thoughts, ask questions, and provide answers. An inadequate vocabulary can impede communication with a foreigner and make it difficult to understand a book or movie well.

The pace of activity in all spheres of modern life, including the learning of modern languages, has increased. Today, we need to memorize large amounts of information (grammar rules, foreign words, etc.) within a short period. However, this does not need to be difficult. All you need to do is to choose the right training materials, learn a few special techniques, and develop your individual training system.

Having a system is critical to the process of language learning. Many people fail to succeed in this regard; they cannot master a foreign language because they fail to follow a system comprised of selecting materials, organizing lessons, arranging new words to be learned, and so on. The lack of a system causes confusion and eventually, lowers self-confidence.

T&P Books' theme-based dictionaries can be included in the list of elements needed for creating an effective system for learning foreign words. These dictionaries were specially developed for learning purposes and are meant to help students effectively memorize words and expand their vocabulary.

Generally speaking, the process of learning words consists of three main elements:

- Reception (creation or acquisition) of a training material, such as a word list
- Work aimed at memorizing new words
- Work aimed at reviewing the learned words, such as self-testing

All three elements are equally important since they determine the quality of work and the final result. All three processes require certain skills and a well-thought-out approach.

New words are often encountered quite randomly when learning a foreign language and it may be difficult to include them all in a unified list. As a result, these words remain written on scraps of paper, in book margins, textbooks, and so on. In order to systematize such words, we have to create and continually update a "book of new words." A paper notebook, a netbook, or a tablet PC can be used for these purposes.

This "book of new words" will be your personal, unique list of words. However, it will only contain the words that you came across during the learning process. For example, you might have written down the words "Sunday," "Tuesday," and "Friday." However, there are additional words for days of the week, for example, "Saturday," that are missing, and your list of words would be incomplete. Using a theme dictionary, in addition to the "book of new words," is a reasonable solution to this problem.

The theme-based dictionary may serve as the basis for expanding your vocabulary.

It will be your big "book of new words" containing the most frequently used words of a foreign language already included. There are quite a few theme-based dictionaries available, and you should ensure that you make the right choice in order to get the maximum benefit from your purchase.

Therefore, we suggest using theme-based dictionaries from T&P Books Publishing as an aid to learning foreign words. Our books are specially developed for effective use in the sphere of vocabulary systematization, expansion and review.

Theme-based dictionaries are not a magical solution to learning new words. However, they can serve as your main database to aid foreign-language acquisition. Apart from theme dictionaries, you can have copybooks for writing down new words, flash cards, glossaries for various texts, as well as other resources; however, a good theme dictionary will always remain your primary collection of words.

T&P Books' theme-based dictionaries are specialty books that contain the most frequently used words in a language.

The main characteristic of such dictionaries is the division of words into themes. For example, the *City* theme contains the words "street," "crossroads," "square," "fountain," and so on. The *Talking* theme might contain words like "to talk," "to ask," "question," and "answer".

All the words in a theme are divided into smaller units, each comprising 3–5 words. Such an arrangement improves the perception of words and makes the learning process less tiresome. Each unit contains a selection of words with similar meanings or identical roots. This allows you to learn words in small groups and establish other associative links that have a positive effect on memorization.

The words on each page are placed in three columns: a word in your native language, its translation, and its transcription. Such positioning allows for the use of techniques for effective memorization. After closing the translation column, you can flip through and review foreign words, and vice versa. "This is an easy and convenient method of review – one that we recommend you do often."

Our theme-based dictionaries contain transcriptions for all the foreign words. Unfortunately, none of the existing transcriptions are able to convey the exact nuances of foreign pronunciation. That is why we recommend using the transcriptions only as a supplementary learning aid. Correct pronunciation can only be acquired with the help of sound. Therefore our collection includes audio theme-based dictionaries.

The process of learning words using T&P Books' theme-based dictionaries gives you the following advantages:

• You have correctly grouped source information, which predetermines your success at subsequent stages of word memorization

• Availability of words derived from the same root (lazy, lazily, lazybones), allowing you to memorize word units instead of separate words

• Small units of words facilitate the process of establishing associative links needed for consolidation of vocabulary

• You can estimate the number of learned words and hence your level of language knowledge

• The dictionary allows for the creation of an effective and high-quality revision process

• You can revise certain themes several times, modifying the revision methods and techniques

• Audio versions of the dictionaries help you to work out the pronunciation of words and develop your skills of auditory word perception

The T&P Books' theme-based dictionaries are offered in several variants differing in the number of words: 1.500, 3.000, 5.000, 7.000, and 9.000 words. There are also dictionaries containing 15,000 words for some language combinations. Your choice of dictionary will depend on your knowledge level and goals.

We sincerely believe that our dictionaries will become your trusty assistant in learning foreign languages and will allow you to easily acquire the necessary vocabulary.

TABLE OF CONTENTS

TRAVEL. HOTEL

TRANSPORT

CITY

CLOTHING & ACCESSORIES

EVERYDAY EXPERIENCE

MEALS. RESTAURANT

PRONUNCIATION GUIDE

Letter	French sample	T&P phonetics alphabet	English sample

Vowels

Letter	French sample	T&P phonetics alphabet	English sample
A a	cravate	[a]	shorter than in ask
E e	mer	[ɛ]	man, bad
I i [1]	hier	[j]	yes, New York
I i [2]	musique	[i]	shorter than in feet
O o	porte	[o], [ɔ]	drop, baught
U u	rue	[y]	fuel, tuna
Y y [3]	yacht	[j]	yes, New York
Y y [4]	type	[i]	shorter than in feet

Consonants

Letter	French sample	T&P phonetics alphabet	English sample
B b	robe	[b]	baby, book
C c [5]	place	[s]	city, boss
C c [6]	canard	[k]	clock, kiss
Ç ç	leçon	[s]	city, boss
D d	disque	[d]	day, doctor
F f	femme	[f]	face, food
G g [7]	page	[ʒ]	forge, pleasure
G g [8]	gare	[g]	game, gold
H h	héros	silent [h]	where
J j	jour	[ʒ]	forge, pleasure
K k	kilo	[k]	clock, kiss
L l	aller	[l]	lace, people
M m	maison	[m]	magic, milk
N n	nom	[n]	name, normal
P p	papier	[p]	pencil, private
Q q	cinq	[k]	clock, kiss
R r	mars	rolled [r]	robot, right
S s [9]	raison	[z]	zebra, please
S s [10]	sac	[s]	city, boss
T t	table	[t]	tourist, trip
V v	verre	[v]	very, river
W w	Taïwan	[w]	vase, winter
X x [11]	expliquer	[ks]	box, taxi
X x [12]	exact	[gz]	exam, exact

Letter	French sample	T&P phonetics alphabet	English sample
X x [13]	dix	[s]	city, boss
X x [14]	dixième	[z]	zebra, please
Z z	zéro	[z]	zebra, please

Combinations of letters

ai	faire	[ɛ]	man, bad
au	faute	[o], [oː]	floor, doctor
ay	payer	[eɪ]	age, today
ei	treize	[ɛ]	man, bad
eau	eau	[o], [oː]	floor, doctor
eu	beurre	[ø]	eternal, church
œ	œil	[ø]	eternal, church
œu	cœur	[øː]	first, thirsty
ou	nous	[u]	book
oi	noir	[wa]	watt, white
oy	voyage	[wa]	watt, white
qu	quartier	[k]	clock, kiss
ch	chat	[ʃ]	machine, shark
th	thé	[t]	tourist, trip
ph	photo	[f]	face, food
gu [15]	guerre	[g]	game, gold
ge [16]	géographie	[ʒ]	forge, pleasure
gn	ligne	[ɲ]	canyon, new
on, om	maison, nom	[ɔ̃]	strong

Comments

[1] before vowels
[2] elsewhere
[3] before vowels
[4] elsewhere
[5] before e, i, y
[6] elsewhere
[7] before e, i, y
[8] elsewhere
[9] between two vowels
[10] elsewhere
[11] most of cases
[12] rarely
[13] in dix, six, soixante
[14] in dixième, sixième
[15] before e, i, u
[16] before a, o, y

ABBREVIATIONS
used in the vocabulary

ab.	-	about
adj	-	adjectif
adv	-	adverb
attr	-	attributive noun
e.g.	-	for example
etc.	-	et cetera
fem.	-	feminine
masc.	-	masculine
noun	-	noun
pl	-	plural
sb	-	somebody
sing.	-	singular
sth	-	something
vi	-	intransitive verb
vi, vt	-	intransitive, transitive verb
vt	-	transitive verb
m	-	masculine
f	-	feminine
m pl	-	masculine plural
f pl	-	feminine plural
m, f	-	masculine, feminine

BASIC CONCEPTS

1. Pronouns

I, me	**je**	[ʒə]
you	**tu**	[ty]
he	**il**	[il]
she	**elle**	[ɛl]
it	**ça**	[sa]
we	**nous**	[nu]
you	**vous**	[vu]
they	**ils**	[il]
they (fem.)	**elles**	[ɛl]
my (masc.)	**mon**	[mɔ̃]
my (fem.)	**ma**	[ma]
my (pl)	**mes**	[me]
your (masc.)	**ton**	[tɔ̃]
your (fem.)	**ta**	[ta]
your (pl)	**tes**	[te]
his	**sa, son**	[sa], [sɔ̃]
her	**sa, son**	[sa], [sɔ̃]
our (masc., sing.)	**notre**	[nɔtr]
our (fem., sing.)	**notre**	[nɔtr]
our (pl)	**nos**	[no]
your (masc., sing.)	**votre**	[vɔtr]
your (fem., sing.)	**votre**	[vɔtr]
your (pl)	**vos**	[vo]
their (sing.)	**leur**	[lœr]
their (pl)	**leurs**	[lœr]

2. Greetings. Salutations

Hello! (familiar)	**Bonjour!**	[bɔ̃ʒur]
Hello! (formal)	**Bonjour!**	[bɔ̃ʒur]
Good morning!	**Bonjour!**	[bɔ̃ʒur]
Good afternoon!	**Bonjour!**	[bɔ̃ʒur]
Good evening!	**Bonsoir!**	[bɔ̃swar]
to say hello	**dire bonjour**	[dir bɔ̃ʒur]
Hi! (hello)	**Salut!**	[saly]

greeting (noun)	salut (m)	[saly]
to greet (vt)	saluer	[salɥe]
How are you?	Comment ça va?	[kɔmɑ̃ sa va]
What's new?	Quoi de neuf?	[kwa də nœf]

Bye-Bye! Goodbye!	Au revoir!	[orəvwar]
See you soon!	À bientôt!	[ɑ bjɛ̃to]
Farewell! (to a friend)	Adieu!	[adjø]
Farewell (formal)	Adieu!	[adjø]
to say goodbye	dire au revoir	[dir orəvwar]
So long!	Salut!	[saly]

Thank you!	Merci!	[mɛrsi]
Thank you very much!	Merci beaucoup!	[mɛrsi boku]
You're welcome	Je vous en prie.	[ʒə vuzɑ̃pri]
Don't mention it!	Pas de quoi.	[pɑ də kwa]
It was nothing	Pas de quoi.	[pɑ də kwa]

Excuse me! (familiar)	Excuse-moi!	[ɛkskyz mwa]
Excuse me! (formal)	Excusez-moi!	[ɛkskyze mwa]
to excuse (forgive)	excuser	[ɛkskyze]

to apologize (vi)	s'excuser	[sɛkskyze]
My apologies	Mes excuses.	[me zɛkskyz]
I'm sorry!	Pardonnez-moi!	[pardɔne mwa]
to forgive (vt)	pardonner	[pardɔne]

| please (adv) | s'il vous plaît | [silvuple] |
| Don't forget! | N'oubliez pas! | [nublije pɑ] |

Certainly!	Bien sûr!	[bjɛ̃ sy:r]
Of course not!	Bien sûr que non!	[bjɛ̃ syr kə nõ]
OK! (I agree)	D'accord!	[dakɔr]
That's enough!	Ça suffit!	[sa syfi]

3. Questions

Who?	Qui?	[ki]
What?	Quoi?	[kwa]
Where? (at, in)	Où?	[u]
Where (to)?	Où?	[u]

Where ... from?	D'où?	[du]
When?	Quand?	[kɑ̃]
Why? (aim)	Pourquoi?	[purkwa]
Why? (reason)	Pourquoi?	[purkwa]

What for?	À quoi bon?	[ɑ kwa bõ]
How? (in what way)	Comment?	[kɔmɑ̃]
What? (which?)	Quel?	[kɛl]

Which?	**Lequel?**	[ləkɛl]
To whom?	**À qui?**	[ɑ ki]
About whom?	**De qui?**	[də ki]
About what?	**De quoi?**	[də kwa]
With whom?	**Avec qui?**	[avɛk ki]
How many? How much?	**Combien?**	[kõbjɛ̃]
Whose?	**À qui?**	[ɑ ki]

4. Prepositions

with (accompanied by)	**avec**	[avɛk]
without	**sans**	[sɑ̃]
to (indicating direction)	**à**	[ɑ]
about (e.g., talking ~ ...)	**de**	[də]
before (in time)	**avant**	[avɑ̃]
in front of ...	**devant**	[dəvɑ̃]
under (beneath, below)	**sous**	[su]
above (in a higher position)	**au-dessus (de ...)**	[odsy də]
on (e.g., ~ the table)	**sur**	[syr]
from (off, out of)	**de**	[də]
of (made from)	**en**	[ɑ̃]
in (e.g., ~ ten minutes)	**dans**	[dɑ̃]
over (across the top of)	**par dessus**	[par dəsy]

5. Function words. Adverbs. Part 1

Where? (at, in)	**Où?**	[u]
here	**ici**	[isi]
there (in a particular place)	**là-bas**	[laba]
somewhere	**quelque part**	[kɛlkə par]
nowhere	**nulle part**	[nyl par]
by (near, beside)	**près**	[prɛ]
by the window	**près de la fenêtre**	[prɛdə la fənɛtr]
Where (to)?	**Où?**	[u]
here (e.g., come ~!)	**ici**	[isi]
there (e.g., to go ~)	**là-bas**	[laba]
from here	**d'ici**	[disi]
from there	**de là-bas**	[də laba]
near (in space)	**près**	[prɛ]
far (distant in space)	**loin**	[lwɛ̃]
near (e.g., ~ Paris)	**à côté**	[ɑkote]
nearby	**près**	[prɛ]

not far	**pas loin**	[pɑ lwɛ̃]
left	**gauche**	[goʃ]
on the left	**à gauche**	[agoʃ]
to the left	**à gauche**	[agoʃ]
right	**droit**	[drwa]
on the right	**à droite**	[adrwat]
to the right	**à droite**	[adrwat]
in front	**devant**	[dəvɑ̃]
front (attr)	**de devant**	[də dəvɑ̃]
ahead (in space)	**en avant**	[ɑn avɑ̃]
behind	**derrière**	[dɛrjɛr]
from behind	**par derrière**	[par dɛrjɛr]
back (towards the rear)	**en arrière**	[ɑn arjɛr]
middle	**milieu** (m)	[miljø]
in the middle	**au milieu**	[omiljø]
at the side	**à côté**	[akote]
everywhere	**partout**	[partu]
around (in all directions)	**autour**	[otur]
from inside	**de l'intérieur**	[də lɛ̃terjœr]
somewhere (to go)	**quelque part**	[kɛlkə par]
straight (directly)	**tout droit**	[tu drwa]
back (e.g., come ~)	**en arrière**	[ɑn arjɛr]
from anywhere	**de quelque part**	[də kɛlkə par]
from somewhere	**de quelque part**	[də kɛlkə par]
firstly	**premièrement**	[prəmjɛrmɑ̃]
secondly	**deuxièmement**	[døzjɛmmɑ̃]
thirdly	**troisièmement**	[trwazjɛmmɑ̃]
suddenly	**soudain**	[sudɛ̃]
at first	**au début**	[odeby]
for the first time	**pour la première fois**	[pur la prəmjɛr fwa]
long before ...	**bien avant ...**	[bjɛn avɑ̃]
anew (over again)	**à nouveau**	[ɑnuvo]
for good	**pour toujours**	[pur tuʒur]
never	**jamais**	[ʒamɛ]
again	**encore**	[ɑ̃kɔr]
now	**maintenant**	[mɛ̃tnɑ̃]
often	**souvent**	[suvɑ̃]
then	**alors**	[alɔr]
urgently (quickly)	**d'urgence**	[dyrʒɑs]
usually	**d'habitude**	[dabityd]
by the way, ...	**à propos, ...**	[aprɔpo]
possible (e.g., that is ~)	**c'est possible**	[sepɔsibl]

probably	probablement	[prɔbabləmɑ̃]
maybe	peut-être	[pøtɛtr]
besides ...	en plus, ...	[ɑ̃plys]
that's why ...	c´est pourquoi ...	[se purkwa]
in spite of ...	malgré ...	[malgre]
thanks to ...	grâce à ...	[gras ɑ]

what (pron.)	quoi	[kwa]
that	que	[kə]
something	quelque chose	[kɛlkə ʃoz]
anything (something)	quelque chose	[kɛlkə ʃoz]
nothing	rien	[rjɛ̃]

who (pron.)	qui	[ki]
someone	quelqu'un	[kɛlkœ̃]
somebody	quelqu'un	[kɛlkœ̃]

nobody	personne	[pɛrsɔn]
nowhere	nulle part	[nyl par]
nobody's	à personne	[ɑ pɛrsɔn]
somebody's	à quelqu'un	[ɑ kɛlkœ̃]

this (neutral)	c'est	[sɛ]
this (masc.)	ce	[sə]
that (neutral)	ce... là	[sə ... la]
that (masc.)	ce... là	[sə ... la]

so (e.g., I'm ~ glad)	comme ça	[kɔmsa]
also (as well)	également	[egalmɑ̃]
too (as well)	aussi	[osi]

6. Function words. Adverbs. Part 2

Why?	Pourquoi?	[purkwa]
for some reason	on ne sait pourquoi	[ɔ̃nə sɛ purkwa]
because ...	parce que ...	[parskə]
for some purpose	on ne sait pourquoi	[ɔ̃nə sɛ purkwa]

and	et	[e]
or	ou	[u]
but	mais	[mɛ]
for (e.g., ~ me)	pour	[pur]

too (excessively)	trop	[tro]
only (exclusively)	seulement	[sœlmɑ̃]
exactly	précisément	[presizemɑ̃]
about (more or less)	autour de ...	[otur də]

| approximately | approximativement | [aprɔksimativmɑ̃] |
| approximate | approximatif | [aprɔksimatif] |

almost	**presque**	[prɛsk]
the rest	**reste** (m)	[rɛst]
other, another	**autre**	[otr]
each	**chaque**	[ʃak]
any (no matter which)	**chacun**	[ʃakœ̃]
many, much (a lot of)	**beaucoup**	[boku]
many people	**plusieurs**	[plyzjœr]
all (everyone)	**tout le monde**	[tu lmɔ̃d]
in exchange for ...	**en échange de ...**	[ɑn eʃɑ̃ʒ də ...]
in exchange	**en échange**	[ɑn eʃɑ̃ʒ]
by hand (made)	**à la main**	[alamɛ̃]
hardly (negative opinion)	**peu probable**	[pø prɔbabl]
probably	**probablement**	[prɔbabləmɑ̃]
on purpose	**exprès**	[ɛksprɛ]
by accident	**par hasard**	[par azar]
very	**très**	[trɛ]
for example	**par exemple**	[par ɛgzɑ̃p]
between	**entre**	[ɑ̃tr]
among	**parmi**	[parmi]
so much (such a lot)	**autant**	[otɑ̃]
especially	**surtout**	[syrtu]

NUMBERS. MISCELLANEOUS

7. Cardinal numbers. Part 1

0 zero	**zéro**	[zero]
1 one	**un**	[œ̃]
2 two	**deux**	[dø]
3 three	**trois**	[trwa]
4 four	**quatre**	[katr]
5 five	**cinq**	[sɛ̃k]
6 six	**six**	[sis]
7 seven	**sept**	[sɛt]
8 eight	**huit**	[ɥit]
9 nine	**neuf**	[nœf]
10 ten	**dix**	[dis]
11 eleven	**onze**	[ɔ̃z]
12 twelve	**douze**	[duz]
13 thirteen	**treize**	[trɛz]
14 fourteen	**quatorze**	[katɔrz]
15 fifteen	**quinze**	[kɛ̃z]
16 sixteen	**seize**	[sɛz]
17 seventeen	**dix-sept**	[disɛt]
18 eighteen	**dix-huit**	[dizɥit]
19 nineteen	**dix-neuf**	[diznœf]
20 twenty	**vingt**	[vɛ̃]
21 twenty-one	**vingt et un**	[vɛ̃teœ̃]
22 twenty-two	**vingt-deux**	[vɛ̃tdø]
23 twenty-three	**vingt-trois**	[vɛ̃trwa]
30 thirty	**trente**	[trɑ̃t]
31 thirty-one	**trente et un**	[trɑ̃teœ̃]
32 thirty-two	**trente-deux**	[trɑ̃t dø]
33 thirty-three	**trente-trois**	[trɑ̃t trwa]
40 forty	**quarante**	[karɑ̃t]
41 forty-one	**quarante et un**	[karɑ̃teœ̃]
42 forty-two	**quarante-deux**	[karɑ̃t dø]
43 forty-three	**quarante-trois**	[karɑ̃t trwa]
50 fifty	**cinquante**	[sɛ̃kɑ̃t]
51 fifty-one	**cinquante et un**	[sɛ̃kɑ̃teœ̃]
52 fifty-two	**cinquante-deux**	[sɛ̃kɑ̃t dø]

53 fifty-three	cinquante-trois	[sɛ̃kɑ̃t trwa]
60 sixty	soixante	[swasɑ̃t]
61 sixty-one	soixante et un	[swasɑ̃teœ̃]
62 sixty-two	soixante-deux	[swasɑ̃t dø]
63 sixty-three	soixante-trois	[swasɑ̃t trwa]

70 seventy	soixante-dix	[swasɑ̃tdis]
71 seventy-one	soixante et onze	[swasɑ̃te ɔ̃z]
72 seventy-two	soixante-douze	[swasɑ̃t duz]
73 seventy-three	soixante-treize	[swasɑ̃t trɛz]

80 eighty	quatre-vingts	[katrəvɛ̃]
81 eighty-one	quatre-vingt et un	[katrəvɛ̃teœ̃]
82 eighty-two	quatre-vingt deux	[katrəvɛ̃ dø]
83 eighty-three	quatre-vingt trois	[katrəvɛ̃ trwa]

90 ninety	quatre-vingt-dix	[katrəvɛ̃dis]
91 ninety-one	quatre-vingt et onze	[katrəvɛ̃ teɔ̃z]
92 ninety-two	quatre-vingt-douze	[katrəvɛ̃ duz]
93 ninety-three	quatre-vingt-treize	[katrəvɛ̃ trɛz]

8. Cardinal numbers. Part 2

100 one hundred	cent	[sɑ̃]
200 two hundred	deux cents	[dø sɑ̃]
300 three hundred	trois cents	[trwa sɑ̃]
400 four hundred	quatre cents	[katr sɑ̃]
500 five hundred	cinq cents	[sɛ̃k sɑ̃]

600 six hundred	six cents	[si sɑ̃]
700 seven hundred	sept cents	[sɛt sɑ̃]
800 eight hundred	huit cents	[ɥi sɑ̃]
900 nine hundred	neuf cents	[nœf sɑ̃]
1000 one thousand	mille	[mil]

2000 two thousand	deux mille	[dø mil]
3000 three thousand	trois mille	[trwa mil]
10000 ten thousand	dix mille	[di mil]
one hundred thousand	cent mille	[sɑ̃ mil]
million	million (m)	[miljɔ̃]
billion	milliard (m)	[miljar]

9. Ordinal numbers

first	premier	[prəmje]
second	deuxième	[døzjɛm]
third	troisième	[trwazjɛm]
fourth	quatrième	[katrijɛm]

fifth	**cinquième**	[sɛ̃kjɛm]
sixth	**sixième**	[sizjɛm]
seventh	**septième**	[sɛtjɛm]
eighth	**huitième**	[ɥitjɛm]
ninth	**neuvième**	[nœvjɛm]
tenth	**dixième**	[dizjɛm]

COLOURS. UNITS OF MEASUREMENT

10. Colors

color	**couleur** (f)	[kulœr]
shade (nuance)	**teinte** (f)	[tɛ̃t]
tone	**ton** (m)	[tɔ̃]
rainbow	**arc-en-ciel** (m)	[arkɑ̃sjɛl]
white	**blanc**	[blɑ̃]
black	**noir**	[nwar]
gray	**gris**	[gri]
green	**vert**	[vɛr]
yellow	**jaune**	[ʒon]
red	**rouge**	[ruʒ]
blue	**bleu**	[blø]
light blue	**bleu clair**	[blø klɛr]
pink	**rose**	[roz]
orange	**orange**	[ɔrɑ̃ʒ]
violet	**violet**	[vjɔlɛ]
brown	**brun**	[brœ̃]
golden	**d'or**	[dɔr]
silvery	**argenté**	[arʒɑ̃te]
beige	**beige**	[bɛʒ]
cream	**crème**	[krɛm]
turquoise	**turquoise**	[tyrkwaz]
cherry	**cerise**	[səriz]
lilac	**lilas**	[lila]
raspberry	**framboise**	[frɑ̃bwaz]
light	**clair**	[klɛr]
dark	**foncé**	[fɔ̃se]
bright	**vif**	[vif]
colored (pencils)	**de couleur**	[də kulœr]
color (e.g., ~ film)	**en couleurs**	[ɑ̃ kulœr]
black-and-white	**noir et blanc**	[nwar e blɑ̃]
plain (one color)	**monochrome**	[mɔnɔkrom]
multicolored	**multicolore**	[myltikɔlɔr]

11. Units of measurement

weight	**poids** (m)	[pwa]
length	**longueur** (f)	[lɔ̃gœr]
width	**largeur** (f)	[larʒœr]
height	**hauteur** (f)	[otœr]
depth	**profondeur** (f)	[prɔfɔ̃dœr]
volume	**volume** (m)	[vɔlym]
area	**surface** (f)	[syrfas]
gram	**gramme** (m)	[gram]
milligram	**milligramme** (m)	[miligram]
kilogram	**kilogramme** (m)	[kilɔgram]
ton	**tonne** (f)	[tɔn]
pound (unit of weight)	**livre** (f)	[livr]
ounce	**once** (f)	[ɔ̃s]
meter	**mètre** (m)	[mɛtr]
millimeter	**millimètre** (m)	[milimɛtr]
centimeter	**centimètre** (m)	[sɑ̃timɛtr]
kilometer	**kilomètre** (m)	[kilɔmɛtr]
mile	**mille** (m)	[mil]
inch	**pouce** (m)	[pus]
foot	**pied** (m)	[pje]
yard	**yard** (m)	[jard]
square meter	**mètre** (m) **carré**	[mɛtr kare]
hectare	**hectare** (m)	[ɛktar]
liter	**litre** (m)	[litr]
degree	**degré** (m)	[dəgre]
volt	**volt** (m)	[vɔlt]
ampere	**ampère** (m)	[ɑ̃pɛr]
horsepower	**cheval-vapeur** (m)	[ʃəvalvapœr]
quantity	**quantité** (f)	[kɑ̃tite]
a little bit of ...	**un peu de ...**	[œ̃ pø də]
half	**moitié** (f)	[mwatje]
dozen	**douzaine** (f)	[duzɛn]
piece (item)	**pièce** (f)	[pjɛs]
size	**dimension** (f)	[dimɑ̃sjɔ̃]
scale (of model, drawing)	**échelle** (f)	[eʃɛl]
minimum	**minimal**	[minimal]
the smallest	**le plus petit**	[lə ply pəti]
medium	**moyen**	[mwajɛ̃]
maximum	**maximal**	[maksimal]
the largest	**le plus grand**	[lə ply grɑ̃]

12. Containers

jar (glass)	**bocal** (m)	[bɔkal]
can	**boîte** (f) **en métal**	[bwat ɑ̃ metal]
bucket	**seau** (m)	[so]
barrel	**tonneau** (m)	[tɔno]

basin (for washing)	**bassine** (f)	[basin]
tank (for liquid, gas)	**réservoir** (m)	[rezɛrvwar]
flask (for water, wine)	**flasque** (f)	[flask]
jerrycan	**jerrycan** (m)	[ʒerikan]
cistern (tank)	**citerne** (f)	[sitɛrn]

mug	**grande tasse** (f)	[grɑ̃d tɑs]
cup (of coffee etc.)	**tasse** (f)	[tɑs]
saucer	**soucoupe** (f)	[sukup]
glass (~ of water)	**verre** (m)	[vɛr]
glass (~ of vine)	**verre** (m)	[vɛr]
stew pot	**casserole** (f)	[kasrɔl]

| bottle (e.g., ~ of wine) | **bouteille** (f) | [butɛj] |
| neck (of the bottle) | **goulot** (m) | [gulo] |

carafe	**carafe** (f)	[karaf]
pitcher (earthenware)	**cruche** (f)	[kryʃ]
vessel (container)	**récipient** (m)	[resipjɑ̃]
pot (pottery object)	**pot** (m)	[po]
vase	**vase** (m)	[vaz]

bottle (e.g., ~ of perfume)	**flacon** (m)	[flakɔ̃]
vial, small bottle	**fiole** (f)	[fjɔl]
tube (of toothpaste)	**tube** (m)	[tyb]

sack (bag)	**sac** (m)	[sak]
bag (paper, plastic)	**sac** (m)	[sak]
package (small parcel)	**paquet** (m)	[pakɛ]
pack (of cigarettes etc.)	**paquet** (m)	[pakɛ]
pack	**emballage** (m)	[ɑ̃balaʒ]

box (e.g., shoebox)	**boîte** (f)	[bwat]
box (for transportation)	**caisse** (f)	[kɛs]
basket (for carrying)	**panier** (m)	[panje]

MAIN VERBS

13. The most important verbs. Part 1

to advise (vt)	**conseiller**	[kɔ̃seje]
to agree (vi, vt)	**accepter**	[aksɛpte]
to answer (vi, vt)	**répondre**	[repɔ̃dr]
to apologize (vi)	**s'excuser**	[sɛkskyze]
to arrive (vi)	**venir**	[vənir]
to ask (~ sb to do sth)	**demander**	[dəmɑ̃de]
to ask (e.g., ~ oneself)	**demander**	[dəmɑ̃de]
to be afraid	**avoir peur**	[avwar pœr]
to be hungry	**avoir faim**	[avwar fɛ̃]
to be interested in …	**s'intéresser**	[sɛ̃terese]
to be necessary	**être nécessaire**	[ɛtr nesesɛr]
to be surprised	**s'étonner**	[setɔne]
to be thirsty	**avoir soif**	[avwar swaf]
to begin (vi, vt)	**commencer**	[kɔmɑ̃se]
to belong to …	**appartenir à …**	[apartənir a]
to boast (vi)	**se vanter**	[sə vɑ̃te]
to break (split into pieces)	**casser**	[kase]
to call (for help)	**appeler**	[aple]
can (modal verb)	**pouvoir**	[puvwar]
to catch (vt)	**attraper**	[atrape]
to change (vt)	**changer**	[ʃɑ̃ʒe]
to choose (select)	**choisir**	[ʃwazir]
to come down	**descendre**	[desɑ̃dr]
to come in (enter)	**entrer**	[ɑ̃tre]
to compare (vt)	**comparer**	[kɔ̃pare]
to complain (vi, vt)	**se plaindre**	[sə plɛ̃dr]
to continue (vi, vt)	**continuer**	[kɔ̃tinɥe]
to control (vt)	**contrôler**	[kɔ̃trole]
to cook (dinner)	**préparer**	[prepare]
to cost (vt)	**coûter**	[kute]
to count (add up)	**compter**	[kɔ̃te]
to count on …	**compter sur …**	[kɔ̃te syr]
to create (vt)	**créer**	[kree]
to cry (weep)	**pleurer**	[plœre]

14. The most important verbs. Part 2

to deceive (vi, vt)	**tromper**	[trɔ̃pe]
to decorate (tree, street)	**décorer**	[dekɔre]
to defend (a country etc.)	**défendre**	[defɑ̃dr]
to demand (request firmly)	**exiger**	[ɛgziʒe]
to dig (vi, vt)	**creuser**	[krøze]
to direct (supervise)	**diriger**	[diriʒe]
to discuss (talk about)	**discuter**	[diskyte]
to do (vt)	**faire**	[fɛr]
to doubt (have doubts)	**douter**	[dute]
to drop (let fall)	**faire tomber**	[fɛr tɔ̃be]
to exist (vi)	**exister**	[ɛgziste]
to expect (foresee)	**prévoir**	[prevwar]
to explain (vi, vt)	**expliquer**	[ɛksplike]
to fall (vi)	**tomber**	[tɔ̃be]
to find (vt)	**trouver**	[truve]
to finish (vt)	**terminer**	[tɛrmine]
to fly (vi)	**voler**	[vɔle]
to follow … (come after)	**suivre**	[sɥivr]
to forget (vi, vt)	**oublier**	[ublije]
to forgive (vt)	**pardonner**	[pardɔne]
to give (vt)	**donner**	[dɔne]
to go (to walk)	**aller**	[ale]
to go for a swim	**se baigner**	[sə beɲe]
to go out	**sortir**	[sɔrtir]
to guess right	**deviner**	[dəvine]
to have (vt)	**avoir**	[avwar]
to have breakfast	**prendre le petit déjeuner**	[prɑ̃dr ləpti deʒœne]
to have dinner	**dîner**	[dine]
to have lunch	**déjeuner**	[deʒœne]
to hear (vi, vt)	**entendre**	[ɑ̃tɑ̃dr]
to help (assist, aid)	**aider**	[ede]
to hide (vt)	**cacher**	[kaʃe]
to hint (vi)	**faire allusion**	[fɛr alyzjɔ̃]
to hope (vi, vt)	**espérer**	[ɛspere]
to hunt (vi, vt)	**chasser**	[ʃase]
to hurry (vi)	**être pressé**	[ɛtr prese]

15. The most important verbs. Part 3

to inform (vi, vt)	**informer**	[ɛ̃fɔrme]
to insist (vi, vt)	**insister**	[ɛ̃siste]

to insult (vt)	**insulter**	[ɛ̃sylte]
to invite (vt)	**inviter**	[ɛ̃vite]
to joke (vi)	**plaisanter**	[plɛzɑ̃te]
to keep (vt)	**garder**	[garde]
to keep silence	**se taire**	[sə tɛr]
to kill (vt)	**tuer**	[tɥe]
to know (sb)	**connaître**	[kɔnɛtr]
to know (sth)	**savoir**	[savwar]
to laugh (vi)	**rire**	[rir]
to liberate (vt)	**libérer**	[libere]
to like (I like ...)	**plaire**	[plɛr]
to look for ... (search)	**chercher**	[ʃɛrʃe]
to love sb	**aimer**	[eme]
to make a mistake	**se tromper**	[sə trɔ̃pe]
to mean (signify)	**signifier**	[siɲifje]
to mention (talk about)	**mentionner**	[mɑ̃sjɔne]
to miss (school etc.)	**manquer**	[mɑ̃ke]
to mix up (confuse)	**confondre**	[kɔ̃fɔ̃dr]
to notice (see)	**apercevoir**	[apɛrsəvwar]
to object (vi, vt)	**objecter**	[ɔbʒɛkte]
to observe (vt)	**observer**	[ɔpsɛrve]
to open (vt)	**ouvrir**	[uvrir]
to order (meal etc.)	**commander**	[kɔmɑ̃de]
to order (military)	**ordonner**	[ɔrdɔne]
to own (possess)	**posséder**	[pɔsede]
to participate (vi)	**participer à ...**	[partisipe a]
to pay (vi, vt)	**payer**	[peje]
to permit (allow)	**permettre**	[pɛrmɛtr]
to plan (vi, vt)	**planifier**	[planifje]
to play (vi, vt)	**jouer**	[ʒwe]
to pray (vi, vt)	**prier**	[prije]
to prefer (vt)	**préférer**	[prefere]
to promise (vt)	**promettre**	[prɔmɛtr]
to pronounce (say)	**prononcer**	[prɔnɔ̃se]
to propose (vt)	**proposer**	[prɔpoze]
to punish (vt)	**punir**	[pynir]
to read (vi, vt)	**lire**	[lir]
to recommend (vt)	**recommander**	[rəkɔmɑ̃de]
to refuse (vi, vt)	**refuser**	[rəfyze]
to regret (be sorry)	**regretter**	[rəgrɛte]
to rent (of a tenant)	**louer**	[lwe]
to repeat (vt)	**répéter**	[repete]
to reserve, to book	**réserver**	[rezɛrve]
to run (vi)	**courir**	[kurir]

16. The most important verbs. Part 4

to save (rescue)	**sauver**	[sove]
to say (e.g., ~ thank you)	**dire**	[dir]
to scold (vt)	**gronder**	[grɔ̃de]
to see (vi, vt)	**voir**	[vwar]
to sell (goods)	**vendre**	[vɑ̃dr]
to send (vt)	**envoyer**	[ɑ̃vwaje]
to shoot (vi)	**tirer**	[tire]
to shout (vi)	**crier**	[krije]
to show (vi, vt)	**montrer**	[mɔ̃tre]
to sign (document)	**signer**	[siɲe]
to sit down (vi)	**s´asseoir**	[saswar]
to smile (vi)	**sourire**	[surir]
to speak (vi, vt)	**parler**	[parle]
to steal (money, etc.)	**voler**	[vɔle]
to stop (cease)	**cesser**	[sese]
to stop (vi)	**s'arrêter**	[sarete]
to study (vt)	**étudier**	[etydje]
to swim (vi)	**nager**	[naʒe]
to take (vt)	**prendre**	[prɑ̃dr]
to think (vi, vt)	**penser**	[pɑ̃se]
to threaten (vt)	**menacer**	[mənase]
to touch (by hands)	**toucher**	[tuʃe]
to translate (word, text)	**traduire**	[traduir]
to trust (vt)	**avoir confiance**	[avwar kɔ̃fjɑ̃s]
to try (attempt)	**essayer**	[eseje]
to turn (change direction)	**tourner**	[turne]
to underestimate (vt)	**sous-estimer**	[suzɛstime]
to understand (vi, vt)	**comprendre**	[kɔ̃prɑ̃dr]
to unite (join)	**réunir**	[reynir]
to wait (vi, vt)	**attendre**	[atɑ̃dr]
to want (wish, desire)	**vouloir**	[vulwar]
to warn (of the danger)	**avertir**	[avɛrtir]
to work (vi)	**travailler**	[travaje]
to write (vi, vt)	**écrire**	[ekrir]
to write down	**noter**	[nɔte]

TIME. CALENDAR

17. Weekdays

Monday	lundi (m)	[lœ̃di]
Tuesday	mardi (m)	[mardi]
Wednesday	mercredi (m)	[mɛrkrədi]
Thursday	jeudi (m)	[ʒødi]
Friday	vendredi (m)	[vãdrədi]
Saturday	samedi (m)	[samdi]
Sunday	dimanche (m)	[dimãʃ]
today	aujourd'hui	[oʒurdɥi]
tomorrow	demain	[dəmɛ̃]
the day after tomorrow	après-demain	[aprɛdmɛ̃]
yesterday	hier	[ijɛr]
the day before yesterday	avant-hier	[avãtjɛr]
day	jour (m)	[ʒur]
workday	jour (m) ouvrable	[ʒur uvrabl]
holiday	jour (m) férié	[ʒur ferje]
day off	jour (m) de repos	[ʒur də rəpo]
weekend	week-end (m)	[wikɛnd]
all day long	toute la journée	[tut la ʒurne]
next day	le lendemain	[lãdmɛ̃]
two days ago	il y a 2 jours	[ilja də ʒur]
the day before	la veille	[la vɛj]
daily	quotidien	[kɔtidjɛ̃]
every day	tous les jours	[tu le ʒur]
week	semaine (f)	[səmɛn]
last week	la semaine dernière	[la səmɛn dɛrnjɛr]
next week	la semaine prochaine	[la səmɛn prɔʃen]
weekly (adj)	hebdomadaire	[ɛbdɔmadɛr]
every week	chaque semaine	[ʃak səmɛn]
twice a week	2 fois par semaine	[dø fwa par səmɛn]
every Tuesday	tous les mardis	[tu le mardi]

18. Hours. Day and night

morning	matin (m)	[matɛ̃]
in the morning	le matin	[lə matɛ̃]
noon, midday	midi (m)	[midi]

in the afternoon	**dans l'après-midi**	[dã laprɛmidi]
evening	**soir** (m)	[swar]
in the evening	**le soir**	[lə swar]
night	**nuit** (f)	[nɥi]
at night	**la nuit**	[la nɥi]
midnight	**minuit** (f)	[minɥi]
second	**seconde** (f)	[səgɔ̃d]
minute	**minute** (f)	[minyt]
hour	**heure** (f)	[œr]
half an hour	**demi-heure** (f)	[dəmijœr]
quarter of an hour	**un quart d'heure**	[œ̃ kar dœr]
fifteen minutes	**quinze minutes**	[kɛ̃z minyt]
24 hours	**vingt-quatre heures**	[vɛ̃tkatr œr]
sunrise	**lever** (m) **du soleil**	[ləve dy sɔlɛj]
dawn	**aube** (f)	[ob]
early morning	**pointe** (f) **du jour**	[pwɛ̃t dy ʒur]
sunset	**coucher** (m) **du soleil**	[kuʃe dy sɔlɛj]
early in the morning	**tôt le matin**	[to lə matɛ̃]
this morning	**ce matin**	[sə matɛ̃]
tomorrow morning	**demain matin**	[dəmɛ̃ matɛ̃]
this afternoon	**cet après-midi**	[sɛt aprɛmidi]
in the afternoon	**dans l'après-midi**	[dã laprɛmidi]
tomorrow afternoon	**demain après-midi**	[dəmɛn aprɛmidi]
tonight (this evening)	**ce soir**	[sə swar]
tomorrow evening	**demain soir**	[dəmɛ̃ swar]
at 3 o'clock sharp	**à 3 heures précises**	[ɑ trwa zœr presiz]
about 4 o'clock	**autour de 4 heures**	[otur də katr œr]
by 12 o'clock	**vers midi**	[vɛr midi]
in 20 minutes	**dans 20 minutes**	[dã vɛ̃ minyt]
in an hour	**dans une heure**	[dãzyn œr]
on time	**à temps**	[ɑ tã]
a quarter of ...	**moins le quart**	[mwɛ̃ lə kar]
within an hour	**en une heure**	[ɑnyn œr]
every 15 minutes	**tous les quarts d'heure**	[tu le kar dœr]
round the clock	**24 heures sur 24**	[vɛ̃tkatr œr syr vɛ̃tkatr]

19. Months. Seasons

January	**janvier** (m)	[ʒɑ̃vje]
February	**février** (m)	[fevrije]
March	**mars** (m)	[mars]
April	**avril** (m)	[avril]

| May | **mai** (m) | [mɛ] |
| June | **juin** (m) | [ʒɥɛ̃] |

July	**juillet** (m)	[ʒɥijɛ]
August	**août** (m)	[ut]
September	**septembre** (m)	[sɛparemɑ̃]
October	**octobre** (m)	[ɔktɔbr]
November	**novembre** (m)	[nɔvɑ̃br]
December	**décembre** (m)	[desɑ̃br]

spring	**printemps** (m)	[prɛ̃tɑ̃]
in spring	**au printemps**	[oprɛ̃tɑ̃]
spring (attr)	**de printemps**	[də prɛ̃tɑ̃]

summer	**été** (m)	[ete]
in summer	**en été**	[ɑn ete]
summer (attr)	**d'été**	[dete]

fall	**automne** (m)	[otɔn]
in the fall	**en automne**	[ɑn otɔn]
fall (attr)	**d'automne**	[dotɔn]

winter	**hiver** (m)	[ivɛr]
in winter	**en hiver**	[ɑn ivɛr]
winter (attr)	**d'hiver**	[divɛr]

month	**mois** (m)	[mwa]
this month	**ce mois**	[sə mwa]
next month	**le mois prochain**	[lə mwa prɔʃɛ̃]
last month	**le mois dernier**	[lə mwa dɛrnje]

a month ago	**il y a un mois**	[ilja œ̃ mwa]
in a month	**dans un mois**	[dɑ̃zœn mwa]
in two months	**dans 2 mois**	[dɑ̃ də mwa]
a whole month	**tout le mois**	[tu lə mwa]
all month long	**tout un mois**	[tutœ̃ mwa]

monthly (~ magazine)	**mensuel**	[mɑ̃sɥɛl]
monthly (adv)	**tous les mois**	[tu le mwa]
every month	**chaque mois**	[ʃak mwa]
twice a month	**2 fois par mois**	[də fwa par mwa]

year	**année** (f)	[ane]
this year	**cette année**	[sɛt ane]
next year	**l'année prochaine**	[lane prɔʃɛn]
last year	**l'année dernière**	[lane dɛrnjɛr]

a year ago	**il y a un an**	[ilja œnɑ̃]
in a year	**dans un an**	[dɑ̃zœn ɑ̃]
in two years	**dans 2 ans**	[dɑ̃ də zɑ̃]
a whole year	**toute l'année**	[tut lane]
all year long	**toute une année**	[tutyn ane]

every year	**chaque année**	[ʃak ane]
annual (adj)	**annuel**	[anɥɛl]
annually	**tous les ans**	[tu lezɑ̃]
4 times a year	**4 fois par an**	[katr fwa parɑ̃]
date (e.g., today's ~)	**date** (f)	[dat]
date (e.g., ~ of birth)	**date** (f)	[dat]
calendar (of dates)	**calendrier** (m)	[kalɑ̃drije]
half a year	**six mois**	[si mwa]
six months	**semestre** (m)	[səmɛstr]
season (summer etc.)	**saison** (f)	[sɛzɔ̃]
century	**siècle** (m)	[sjɛkl]

TRAVEL. HOTEL

20. Trip. Travel

tourism	**tourisme** (m)	[turism]
tourist	**touriste** (m)	[turist]
trip, voyage	**voyage** (m)	[vwajaʒ]
adventure	**aventure** (f)	[avãtyr]
trip, journey	**voyage** (m)	[vwajaʒ]
vacation	**vacances** (f pl)	[vakãs]
to be on vacation	**être en vacances**	[ɛtr ã vakãs]
rest	**repos** (m)	[rəpo]
train	**train** (m)	[trɛ̃]
by train	**en train**	[ã trɛ̃]
airplane	**avion** (m)	[avjɔ̃]
by airplane	**en avion**	[ɑn avjɔ̃]
by car	**en voiture**	[ã vwatyr]
by ship	**en bateau**	[ã bato]
luggage	**bagage** (m)	[bagaʒ]
suitcase, luggage	**malle** (f)	[mal]
luggage cart	**chariot** (m)	[ʃarjo]
passport	**passeport** (m)	[pɑspɔr]
visa	**visa** (m)	[viza]
ticket	**ticket** (m)	[tikɛ]
air ticket	**billet** (m) **d'avion**	[bijɛ davjɔ̃]
guidebook	**guide** (m)	[gid]
map	**carte** (f)	[kart]
area (place)	**lieu** (m)	[ljø]
place, site	**endroit** (m)	[ãdrwa]
exotica	**exotisme** (m)	[ɛgzɔtism]
exotic	**exotique**	[ɛgzɔtik]
amazing	**étonnant**	[etɔnã]
group	**groupe** (m)	[grup]
excursion	**excursion** (f)	[ɛkskyrsjɔ̃]
guide (person)	**guide** (m)	[gid]

21. Hotel

hotel, motel	**hôtel** (m)	[otɛl]
motel	**motel** (m)	[mɔtɛl]
three-star	**3 étoiles**	[trwa zetwal]
five-star	**5 étoiles**	[sɛ̃k etwal]
to stay (in hotel etc.)	**descendre**	[desɑ̃dr]
room	**chambre** (f)	[ʃɑ̃br]
single room	**chambre** (f) **single**	[ʃɑ̃br siŋgəl]
double room	**chambre** (f) **double**	[ʃɑ̃br dubl]
to book a room	**réserver une chambre**	[rezɛrve yn ʃɑ̃br]
half board	**demi-pension** (f)	[dəmipɑ̃sjɔ̃]
full board	**pension** (f) **complète**	[pɑ̃sjɔ̃ kɔ̃plɛt]
with bath	**avec une salle de bain**	[avɛk yn saldəbɛ̃]
with shower	**avec une douche**	[avɛk yn duʃ]
satellite television	**télévision** (f) **par satellite**	[televizjɔ̃ par satelit]
air-conditioner	**air** (m) **conditionné**	[ɛr kɔ̃disjone]
towel	**serviette** (f)	[sɛrvjɛt]
key	**clé** (f), **clef** (f)	[kle]
administrator	**administrateur** (m)	[administratœr]
chambermaid	**femme** (f) **de chambre**	[fam də ʃɑ̃br]
porter, bellboy	**porteur** (m)	[pɔrtœr]
doorman	**portier** (m)	[pɔrtje]
restaurant	**restaurant** (m)	[rɛstɔrɑ̃]
pub, bar	**bar** (m)	[bar]
café	**café** (m)	[kafe]
breakfast	**petit déjeuner** (m)	[pəti deʒœne]
dinner	**dîner** (m)	[dine]
buffet	**buffet** (m)	[byfɛ]
lobby	**vestibule** (m)	[vɛstibyl]
elevator	**ascenseur** (m)	[asɑ̃sœr]
DO NOT DISTURB	**PRIÈRE** **DE NE PAS DÉRANGER**	[prijɛr dənəpɑ derɑ̃ʒe]
NO SMOKING	**DÉFENSE DE FUMER**	[defɑ̃s də fyme]

22. Sightseeing

monument	**monument** (m)	[mɔnymɑ̃]
fortress	**forteresse** (f)	[fɔrtərɛs]
palace	**palais** (m)	[palɛ]
castle	**château** (m)	[ʃato]

tower	**tour** (f)	[tur]
mausoleum	**mausolée** (m)	[mozɔle]
architecture	**architecture** (f)	[arʃitɛktyr]
medieval	**de Moyen Âge**	[də mwajɛnɑʒ]
ancient	**ancien**	[ãsjɛ̃]
national	**national**	[nasjɔnal]
famous	**connu**	[kɔny]
tourist	**touriste** (m)	[turist]
guide (person)	**guide** (m)	[gid]
excursion (organized trip)	**excursion** (f)	[ɛkskyrsjɔ̃]
to show (vt)	**montrer**	[mɔ̃tre]
to tell (vi, vt)	**raconter**	[rakɔ̃te]
to find (vt)	**trouver**	[truve]
to get lost	**se perdre**	[sə pɛrdr]
map (e.g., subway ~)	**plan** (m)	[plɑ̃]
map (e.g., city ~)	**carte** (f)	[kart]
souvenir, gift	**souvenir** (m)	[suvnir]
gift shop	**boutique** (f) **de souvenirs**	[butik də suvnir]
to take pictures	**photographier**	[fotografje]

TRANSPORT

23. Airport

airport	**aéroport** (m)	[aeropɔr]
airplane	**avion** (m)	[avjɔ̃]
airline	**compagnie** (f) **aérienne**	[kɔ̃paɲi aerjɛn]
air-traffic controller	**aiguilleur** (m) **du ciel**	[eguijœr dy sjɛl]
departure	**départ** (m)	[depar]
arrival	**arrivée** (f)	[arive]
to arrive (vi)	**arriver**	[arive]
departure time	**temps** (m) **de départ**	[tɑ̃ də depar]
arrival time	**temps** (m) **d'arrivée**	[tɑ̃ darive]
to be delayed	**être retardé**	[ɛtr rətarde]
flight delay	**retard** (m) **de l´avion**	[rətar də lavjɔ̃]
information board	**tableau** (m) **d'informations**	[tablo dɛ̃fɔrmasjɔ̃]
information	**information** (f)	[ɛ̃fɔrmasjɔ̃]
to announce (vt)	**annoncer**	[anɔ̃se]
flight (e.g., next ~)	**vol** (m)	[vɔl]
customs	**douane** (f)	[dwan]
customs officer	**douanier** (m)	[dwanje]
declaration	**déclaration** (f)	[deklarasjɔ̃]
to fill out a declaration	**remplir la déclaration**	[rɑ̃plir la deklarasjɔ̃]
passport control	**contrôle** (m) **de passeport**	[kɔ̃trol də paspɔr]
luggage	**bagage** (m)	[bagaʒ]
hand luggage	**bagage** (m) **à main**	[bagaʒ ɑ mɛ̃]
LOST-AND-FOUND	**objets** (m pl) **trouvés**	[ɔbʒɛ truve]
luggage cart	**chariot** (m)	[ʃarjo]
landing	**atterrissage** (m)	[aterisaʒ]
runway	**piste** (f) **d'atterrissage**	[pist daterisaʒ]
to land (vi)	**atterrir**	[aterir]
airstairs	**escalier** (m) **d'avion**	[ɛskalje davjɔ̃]
check-in	**enregistrement** (m)	[ɑ̃rəʒistrəmɑ̃]
check-in desk	**comptoir** (m) **d'enregistrement**	[kɔ̃twar dɑ̃rəʒistrəmɑ̃]

to check-in (vi)	s'enregistrer	[sãrəʒistre]
boarding pass	carte (f) d'embarquement	[kart dãbarkəmã]
departure gate	porte (f) d'embarquement	[pɔrt dãbarkəmã]
transit	transit (m)	[trãzit]
to wait (vi, vt)	attendre	[atãdr]
waiting room	salle (f) d'attente	[sal datãt]
to see off	accompagner	[akɔ̃paɲe]
to say goodbye	faire ses adieux	[fɛr sezadjø]

24. Airplane

airplane	avion (m)	[avjɔ̃]
air ticket	billet (m) d'avion	[bijɛ davjɔ̃]
airline	compagnie (f) aérienne	[kɔ̃paɲi aerjɛn]
airport	aéroport (m)	[aeropɔr]
supersonic	supersonique	[sypɛrsɔnik]
captain	commandant (m) de bord	[kɔmãdã də bɔr]
crew	équipage (m)	[ekipaʒ]
pilot	pilote (m)	[pilɔt]
flight attendant	hôtesse (f) de l'air	[otɛs də lɛr]
navigator	navigateur (m)	[navigatœr]
wings	ailes (f pl)	[ɛl]
tail	queue (f)	[kø]
cockpit	cabine (f)	[kabin]
engine	moteur (m)	[mɔtœr]
undercarriage	train (m) d'atterrissage	[trɛ̃ daterisaʒ]
turbine	turbine (f)	[tyrbin]
propeller	hélice (f)	[elis]
black box	boîte (f) noire	[bwat nwar]
control column	gouvernail (m)	[guvɛrnaj]
fuel	carburant (m)	[karbyrã]
instructions	consigne (f)	[kɔ̃siɲ]
oxygen mask	masque (m) à oxygène	[mask ɑ ɔksiʒɛn]
uniform	uniforme (f)	[ynifɔrm]
life vest	gilet (m) de sauvetage	[ʒilɛ də sovtaʒ]
parachute	parachute (m)	[paraʃyt]
takeoff	décollage (m)	[dekɔlaʒ]
to take off (vi)	décoller	[dekɔle]
runway	piste (f) de décollage	[pist dekɔlaʒ]
visibility	visibilité (f)	[vizibilite]
flight (act of flying)	vol (m)	[vɔl]
altitude	altitude (f)	[altityd]
air pocket	trou (m) d'air	[tru dɛr]

seat	place (f)	[plas]
headphones	écouteurs (m pl)	[ekutœr]
folding tray	tablette (f)	[tablɛt]
window (in plane)	hublot (m)	[yblo]
aisle	couloir (m)	[kulwar]

25. Train

train	train (m)	[trɛ̃]
suburban train	train (m) de banlieue	[trɛ̃ də bɑ̃ljø]
fast train	TGV (m)	[teʒeve]
diesel locomotive	locomotive (f) diesel	[lɔkɔmɔtiv djezɛl]
steam engine	locomotive (f) à vapeur	[lɔkɔmɔtiv a vapœr]

| passenger car | wagon (m) | [vagɔ̃] |
| dining car | wagon-restaurant (m) | [vagɔ̃rɛstɔrɑ̃] |

rails	rails (m pl)	[raj]
railroad	chemin (m) de fer	[ʃəmɛ̃ də fɛr]
railway tie	traverse (f)	[travɛrs]

platform (railway ~)	quai (m)	[kɛ]
platform (e.g., ~ 1, 2 etc.)	voie (f)	[vwa]
semaphore	sémaphore (m)	[semafɔr]
station	station (f)	[stasjɔ̃]

engineer	conducteur (m)	[kɔ̃dyktœr]
porter (of luggage)	porteur (m)	[pɔrtœr]
train steward	steward (m)	[stiwart]
passenger	passager (m)	[pasaʒe]
conductor	contrôleur (m)	[kɔ̃trolœr]

| corridor (in train) | couloir (m) | [kulwar] |
| emergency break | frein (m) d'urgence | [frɛ̃ dyrʒɑ̃s] |

compartment	compartiment (m)	[kɔ̃partimɑ̃]
berth	couchette (f)	[kuʃɛt]
upper berth	couchette (f) d´en haut	[kuʃɛt dɛ̃ o]
lower berth	couchette (f) d´en bas	[kuʃɛt dɛ̃ba]
linen	linge (m)	[lɛ̃ʒ]

ticket	ticket (m)	[tikɛ]
schedule	horaire (m)	[ɔrɛr]
timetable	tableau (m)	[tablo]

to leave, to depart	partir	[partir]
departure	départ (m)	[depar]
to arrive (about train)	arriver	[arive]
arrival	arrivée (f)	[arive]
to be late (about train)	être en retard	[ɛtr ɑ̃ rətar]

to arrive by train	**arriver en train**	[arive ɑ̃ trɛ̃]
to get on the train	**prendre le train**	[prɑ̃dr lə trɛ̃]
to get off the train	**descendre du train**	[desɑ̃dr dy trɛ̃]
train wreck	**accident** (m)	[aksidɑ̃]
steam engine	**locomotive** (f) **à vapeur**	[lɔkɔmɔtiv ɑ vapœr]
stoker, fireman	**chauffeur** (m)	[ʃofœr]
firebox	**chauffe** (f)	[ʃof]
coal	**charbon** (m)	[ʃarbɔ̃]

26. Ship

ship	**bateau** (m)	[bato]
vessel	**navire** (m)	[navir]
steamship	**bateau** (m) **à vapeur**	[bato ɑ vapœr]
riverboat	**paquebot** (m)	[pakbo]
ocean liner	**bateau** (m) **de croisière**	[bato də krwazjɛr]
cruiser	**croiseur** (m)	[krwazœr]
yacht	**yacht** (m)	[jot]
tug	**remorqueur** (m)	[rəmɔrkœr]
barge	**péniche** (f)	[peniʃ]
ferry	**bac** (m)	[bak]
sailing ship	**voilier** (m)	[vwalje]
brigantine	**brigantin** (m)	[brigɑ̃tɛ̃]
ice breaker	**brise-glace** (m)	[brizglas]
submarine	**sous-marin** (m)	[sumarɛ̃]
boat	**barque** (f)	[bark]
dinghy	**canot** (m)	[kano]
lifeboat	**canot** (m) **de sauvetage**	[kano də sovtaʒ]
motorboat	**canot** (m) **à moteur**	[kano ɑ mɔtœr]
captain	**capitaine** (m)	[kapitɛn]
seaman	**matelot** (m)	[matlo]
sailor	**marin** (m)	[marɛ̃]
crew	**équipage** (m)	[ekipaʒ]
boatswain	**maître** (m) **d'équipage**	[mɛtr dekipaʒ]
ship's boy	**mousse** (m)	[mus]
cook	**cuisinier** (m) **du bord**	[kɥizinje dy bɔr]
ship's doctor	**médecin** (m) **de bord**	[medsɛ̃ də bɔr]
deck	**pont** (m)	[pɔ̃]
mast	**mât** (m)	[mɑ]
sail	**voile** (f)	[vwal]
hold	**cale** (f)	[kal]

bow	**proue** (f)	[pʀu]
stern	**poupe** (f)	[pup]
oar	**rame** (f)	[ʀam]
propeller	**hélice** (f)	[elis]

cabin	**cabine** (f)	[kabin]
wardroom	**carré** (m) **des officiers**	[kaʀe dezɔfisje]
engine room	**salle** (f) **des machines**	[sal de maʃin]
the bridge	**passerelle** (f)	[pɑsʀɛl]
radio room	**cabine** (f) **de T.S.F.**	[kabin də teɛsɛf]
wave (radio)	**onde** (f)	[ɔ̃d]
logbook	**journal** (m) **de bord**	[ʒuʀnal də bɔʀ]

spyglass	**longue-vue** (f)	[lɔ̃gvy]
bell	**cloche** (f)	[klɔʃ]
flag	**pavillon** (m)	[pavijɔ̃]

rope (mooring ~)	**amarre** (f)	[amaʀ]
cable (mooring ~)	**câble** (m)	[kabl]
knot (bowline etc.)	**nœud** (m) **marin**	[nø maʀɛ̃]

| handrail | **rampe** (f) | [ʀɑ̃p] |
| gangway | **passerelle** (f) | [pɑsʀɛl] |

anchor	**ancre** (f)	[ɑ̃kʀ]
to weigh anchor	**lever l'ancre**	[ləve lɑ̃kʀ]
to drop anchor	**jeter l'ancre**	[ʒəte lɑ̃kʀ]
anchor chain	**chaîne** (f) **d'ancrage**	[ʃɛn dɑ̃kʀaʒ]

port (harbor)	**port** (m)	[pɔʀ]
wharf, quay	**embarcadère** (m)	[ɑ̃baʀkadɛʀ]
to berth	**se mettre a quai**	[sə mɛtʀ a kɛ]
to cast off	**démarrer**	[demaʀe]

trip (voyage)	**voyage** (m)	[vwajaʒ]
cruise (sea trip)	**croisière** (f)	[kʀwazjɛʀ]
course	**cap** (m)	[kap]
route (itinerary)	**itinéraire** (m)	[itineʀɛʀ]

fairway	**partie** (f) **navigable**	[paʀti navigabl]
shallows	**bas-fond** (m)	[bafɔ̃]
to run aground	**échouer sur un bas-fond**	[eʃwe syʀ œ̃ bafɔ̃]

storm	**tempête** (f)	[tɑ̃pɛt]
signal	**signal** (m)	[siɲal]
to sink (about boat)	**sombrer**	[sɔ̃bʀe]
SOS	**SOS** (m)	[ɛsoɛs]
life buoy	**bouée** (f) **de sauvetage**	[bwe də sovtaʒ]

CITY

27. Urban transport

bus	**autobus** (m)	[otobys]
streetcar	**tramway** (m)	[tramwɛ]
trolley	**trolleybus** (m)	[trɔlɛbys]
route (for buses)	**itinéraire** (m)	[itinerɛr]
number (e.g., bus ~)	**numéro** (m)	[nymero]
to go by …	**prendre** …	[prãdr]
to get on (~ the bus etc.)	**monter**	[mɔ̃te]
to get off …	**descendre de** …	[desãdr də]
to get out (vi)	**descendre de** …	[desãdr də]
stop (e.g., bus ~)	**arrêt** (m)	[arɛ]
next stop	**arrêt** (m) **prochain**	[arɛt prɔʃɛ̃]
terminus	**terminus** (m)	[tɛrminys]
schedule	**horaire** (m)	[ɔrɛr]
to wait (vi, vt)	**attendre**	[atãdr]
ticket	**ticket** (m)	[tikɛ]
fare (charge for bus etc.)	**prix** (m) **du ticket**	[pri dy tikɛ]
cashier	**caissier** (m)	[kesje]
ticket inspection	**contrôle** (m) **des tickets**	[kɔ̃trol de tikɛ]
conductor	**contrôleur** (m)	[kɔ̃trolœr]
to be late (for …)	**être en retard**	[ɛtr ã rətar]
to miss … (the train etc.)	**manquer**	[mãke]
to be in a hurry	**être pressé**	[ɛtr prese]
taxi, cab	**taxi** (m)	[taksi]
taxi driver	**chauffeur** (m) **de taxi**	[ʃofœr də taksi]
by taxi	**en taxi**	[ã taksi]
taxi stand	**arrêt** (m) **de taxi**	[arɛ də taksi]
to call a taxi	**appeler un taxi**	[aple œ̃ taksi]
to take a taxi	**prendre un taxi**	[prãdr œ̃ taksi]
traffic	**trafic** (m)	[trafik]
traffic jam	**embouteillage** (m)	[ãbutɛjaʒ]
rush hour	**heures** (pl) **de pointe**	[œr də pwɛ̃t]
to park (vi)	**se garer**	[sə gare]
to park (vt)	**garer**	[gare]
parking lot	**parking** (m)	[parkiŋ]
subway	**métro** (m)	[metro]

station	**station** (f)	[stasjɔ̃]
to take the subway	**prendre le métro**	[prɑ̃dr lə metro]
train	**train** (m)	[trɛ̃]
train station	**gare** (f)	[gar]

28. City. Life in the city

city, town	**ville** (f)	[vil]
capital	**capitale** (f)	[kapital]
village (e.g., fishing ~)	**village** (m)	[vilaʒ]
small town	**cité** (f)	[site]
city map	**plan** (m) **de la ville**	[plɑ̃ də la vil]
downtown	**centre-ville** (m)	[sɑ̃trəvil]
suburb	**banlieue** (f)	[bɑ̃ljø]
suburban	**de banlieue**	[də bɑ̃ljø]
outskirts	**périphérie** (f)	[periferi]
environs (suburbs)	**alentours** (m pl)	[alɑ̃tur]
district (of city)	**arrondissement** (m)	[arɔ̃dismɑ̃]
block	**quartier** (m)	[kartje]
residential block	**quartier** (m) **résidentiel**	[kartje rezidɑ̃sjɛl]
traffic	**trafic** (m)	[trafik]
traffic lights	**feux** (m pl)	[fø]
public transportation	**transport** (m) **urbain**	[trɑ̃spɔr yrbɛ̃]
intersection	**carrefour** (m)	[karfur]
crosswalk	**passage** (m)	[pɑsaʒ]
pedestrian underpass	**passage** (m) **souterrain**	[pɑsaʒ sutɛrɛ̃]
to cross (vt)	**traverser**	[travɛrse]
pedestrian	**piéton** (m)	[pjetɔ̃]
sidewalk	**trottoir** (m)	[trotwar]
bridge	**pont** (m)	[pɔ̃]
bank, quay	**quai** (m)	[kɛ]
fountain	**fontaine** (f)	[fɔ̃tɛn]
alley (in park, garden)	**allée** (f)	[ale]
park	**parc** (m)	[park]
boulevard	**boulevard** (m)	[bulvar]
square	**place** (f)	[plas]
avenue (wide street)	**avenue** (f)	[avny]
street	**rue** (f)	[ry]
lane	**ruelle** (f)	[rɥɛl]
dead end	**impasse** (f)	[ɛ̃pas]
house	**maison** (f)	[mɛzɔ̃]
building	**édifice** (m)	[edifis]
skyscraper	**gratte-ciel** (m)	[gratsjɛl]

facade	**façade** (f)	[fasad]
roof	**toit** (m)	[twa]
window	**fenêtre** (f)	[fənɛtr]
arch	**arc** (m)	[ark]
column	**colonne** (f)	[kɔlɔn]
corner	**coin** (m)	[kwɛ̃]
store window	**vitrine** (f)	[vitrin]
sign (on shop, bar etc.)	**enseigne** (f)	[ãsɛɲ]
poster	**affiche** (f)	[afiʃ]
advertising poster	**affiche** (f) **publicitaire**	[afiʃ pyblisitɛr]
billboard	**panneau-réclame** (m)	[pano reklam]
garbage, trash	**ordures** (f pl)	[ɔrdyr]
garbage can	**poubelle** (f)	[pubɛl]
to litter (vi)	**jeter qch à terre**	[ʒəte … ɑ tɛr]
garbage dump	**décharge** (f)	[deʃarʒ]
phone booth	**cabine** (f) **téléphonique**	[kabin telefɔnik]
lightpost	**réverbère** (m)	[revɛrbɛr]
bench (park ~)	**banc** (m)	[bã]
policeman	**policier** (m)	[pɔlisje]
police	**police** (f)	[pɔlis]
beggar	**clochard** (m)	[klɔʃar]
homeless, bum	**sans-abri** (m)	[sãzabri]

29. Urban institutions

store	**magasin** (m)	[magazɛ̃]
drugstore, pharmacy	**pharmacie** (f)	[farmasi]
optical store	**opticien** (m)	[ɔptisjɛ̃]
shopping mall	**centre** (m) **commercial**	[sãtr kɔmɛrsjal]
supermarket	**supermarché** (m)	[sypɛrmarʃe]
bakery	**boulangerie** (f)	[bulãʒri]
baker	**boulanger** (m)	[bulãʒe]
confectionery	**pâtisserie** (f)	[pɑtisri]
grocery store	**épicerie** (f)	[episri]
butcher shop	**boucherie** (f)	[buʃri]
produce store	**magasin** (m) **de légumes**	[magazɛ̃ də legym]
market	**marché** (m)	[marʃe]
coffee house	**café** (m)	[kafe]
restaurant	**restaurant** (m)	[rɛstɔrã]
pub	**brasserie** (f)	[brasri]
pizzeria	**pizzeria** (f)	[pidzerja]
hair salon	**salon** (m) **de coiffure**	[salɔ̃ də kwafyr]
post office	**poste** (f)	[pɔst]

dry cleaners	**pressing** (m)	[presiŋ]
photo studio	**atelier** (m) **de photo**	[atəlje də fɔto]
shoe store	**magasin** (m) **de chaussures**	[magazɛ̃ də ʃosyr]
bookstore	**librairie** (f)	[librɛri]
sporting goods store	**magasin** (m) **d'articles de sport**	[magazɛ̃ dartikl də spɔr]
clothes repair	**atelier** (m) **de retouche**	[atəlje də rətuʃ]
formal wear rental	**location** (f) **de vêtements**	[lɔkasjɔ̃ də vɛtmã]
movie rental store	**location** (f) **de films**	[lɔkasjɔ̃ də film]
circus	**cirque** (m)	[sirk]
zoo	**zoo** (m)	[zoo]
movie theater	**cinéma** (m)	[sinema]
museum	**musée** (m)	[myze]
library	**bibliothèque** (f)	[biblijɔtɛk]
theater	**théâtre** (m)	[teɑtr]
opera house	**opéra** (m)	[ɔpera]
nightclub	**boîte** (f) **de nuit**	[bwat də nɥi]
casino	**casino** (m)	[kazino]
mosque	**mosquée** (f)	[mɔske]
synagogue	**synagogue** (f)	[sinagɔg]
cathedral	**cathédrale** (f)	[katedral]
temple	**temple** (m)	[tãpl]
church	**église** (f)	[egliz]
institute	**institut** (m)	[ɛ̃stity]
university	**université** (f)	[ynivɛrsite]
school	**école** (f)	[ekɔl]
prefecture	**préfecture** (f)	[prefɛktyr]
city hall	**mairie** (f)	[meri]
hotel	**hôtel** (m)	[otɛl]
bank	**banque** (f)	[bɑ̃k]
embassy	**ambassade** (f)	[ɑ̃basad]
travel agency	**agence** (f) **de voyages**	[aʒɑ̃s də vwajaʒ]
information office	**bureau** (m) **d'information**	[byro dɛ̃fɔrmasjɔ̃]
money exchange	**bureau** (m) **de change**	[byro də ʃɑ̃ʒ]
subway	**métro** (m)	[metro]
hospital	**hôpital** (m)	[ɔpital]
gas station	**station-service** (f)	[stasjɔ̃sɛrvis]
parking lot	**parking** (m)	[parkiŋ]

30. Signs

sign (on shop, bar etc.)	enseigne (f)	[ɑ̃sɛɲ]
inscription (plaque etc.)	inscription (f)	[ɛ̃skripsjɔ̃]
poster	placard (m)	[plakar]
direction sign	indicateur (m) de direction	[ɛ̃dikatœr də dirɛksjɔ̃]
arrow (direction sign)	flèche (f)	[flɛʃ]
caution	avertissement (m)	[avɛrtismɑ̃]
warning	avertissement (m)	[avɛrtismɑ̃]
to warn (of the danger)	avertir	[avɛrtir]
day off	jour (m) de repos	[ʒur də rəpo]
timetable (schedule)	horaire (m)	[ɔrɛr]
opening hours	heures (pl) d'ouverture	[zœr duvɛrtyr]
WELCOME!	BIENVENUE!	[bjɛ̃vny]
ENTRANCE	ENTRÉE	[ɑ̃tre]
EXIT	SORTIE	[sɔrti]
PUSH	POUSSER	[puse]
PULL	TIRER	[tire]
OPEN	OUVERT	[uvɛr]
CLOSED	FERMÉ	[fɛrme]
WOMEN	FEMMES	[fam]
MEN	HOMMES	[ɔm]
DISCOUNTS	RABAIS	[sɔld]
SALE	SOLDES	[rabɛ]
NEW!	NOUVEAU!	[nuvo]
FREE	GRATUIT	[gratɥi]
ATTENTION!	ATTENTION!	[atɑ̃sjɔ̃]
NO VACANCIES	COMPLET	[kɔ̃plɛ]
RESERVED	RÉSERVÉ	[rezɛrve]
ADMINISTRATION	ADMINISTRATION	[administrasjɔ̃]
BEWARE OF THE DOG!	ATTENTION CHIEN MÉCHANT	[atɑ̃sjɔ̃ ʃjɛ̃ meʃɑ̃]
NO SMOKING	DÉFENSE DE FUMER	[defɑ̃s də fyme]
DO NOT TOUCH!	PRIERE DE NE PAS TOUCHER	[prijɛr dənəpɑ tuʃe]
DANGEROUS	DANGEREUX	[dɑ̃ʒrø]
DANGER	DANGER	[dɑ̃ʒe]
HIGH TENSION	HAUTE TENSION	[ot tɑ̃sjɔ̃]
NO SWIMMING!	BAIGNADE INTERDITE	[bɛɲad ɛ̃tɛrdit]
OUT OF ORDER	HORS SERVICE	[ɔr sɛrvis]

FLAMMABLE	**INFLAMMABLE**	[ɛ̃flamabl]
FORBIDDEN	**INTERDIT**	[ɛ̃tɛrdi]
NO TRESPASSING!	**PASSAGE INTERDIT**	[pɑsaʒ ɛ̃tɛrdi]
WET PAINT	**PEINTURE FRAÎCHE**	[pɛ̃tyr frɛʃ]

31. Shopping

to buy (purchase)	**acheter**	[aʃte]
purchase	**achat** (m)	[aʃa]
to go shopping	**faire des achats**	[fɛr dezaʃa]
shopping	**shopping** (m)	[ʃɔpiŋ]
to be open	**être ouvert**	[ɛtr uvɛr]
to be closed	**être fermé**	[ɛtr fɛrme]
footwear	**chaussures** (f pl)	[ʃosyr]
clothes, clothing	**vêtement** (m)	[vɛtmɑ̃]
cosmetics	**produits** (m pl) **de beauté**	[prɔdyi də bote]
food	**produits** (m pl) **alimentaires**	[prɔdyi alimɑ̃tɛr]
gift, present	**cadeau** (m)	[kado]
salesman	**vendeur** (m)	[vɑ̃dœr]
saleswoman	**vendeuse** (f)	[vɑ̃døz]
check out, cash desk	**caisse** (f)	[kɛs]
mirror	**glace** (f)	[glas]
counter (in shop)	**comptoir** (m)	[kɔ̃twar]
fitting room	**cabine** (f) **d´essayage**	[kabin desɛjaʒ]
to try on	**essayer**	[eseje]
to fit (about dress etc.)	**aller bien**	[ale bjɛ̃]
to like (I like ...)	**plaire à ...**	[plɛr ɑ]
price	**prix** (m)	[pri]
price tag	**étiquette** (f)	[etikɛt]
to cost (vt)	**coûter**	[kute]
How much?	**Combien?**	[kɔ̃bjɛ̃]
discount	**rabais** (m)	[rabɛ]
inexpensive	**pas cher**	[pɑ ʃɛr]
cheap (inexpensive)	**bon marché**	[bɔ̃ marʃe]
expensive	**cher**	[ʃɛr]
It's expensive	**C'est cher.**	[sɛ ʃɛr]
rental (noun)	**location** (f)	[lɔkasjɔ̃]
to rent (~ a tuxedo)	**louer**	[lwe]
credit	**crédit** (m)	[kredi]
on credit	**à crédit**	[ɑkredi]

CLOTHING & ACCESSORIES

32. Outerwear. Coats

clothes	**vêtement** (m)	[vɛtmɑ̃]
outer clothing	**survêtement** (m)	[syrvɛtmɑ̃]
winter clothing	**vêtement** (m) **d'hiver**	[vɛtmɑ̃ divɛr]
overcoat	**manteau** (m)	[mɑ̃to]
fur coat	**manteau** (m) **de fourrure**	[mɑ̃to də furyr]
short fur coat	**veste** (f) **en fourrure**	[vɛst ɑ̃ furyr]
down coat	**manteau** (m) **de duvet**	[manto də dyvɛ]
jacket (e.g., leather ~)	**veste** (f)	[vɛst]
raincoat	**pardessus** (m)	[pardəsy]
waterproof	**imperméable**	[ɛ̃pɛrmeabl]

33. Men's & women's clothing

shirt	**chemise** (f)	[ʃəmiz]
pants	**pantalon** (m)	[pɑ̃talɔ̃]
jeans	**jean** (m)	[dʒin]
jacket (of man's suit)	**veston** (m)	[vɛstɔ̃]
suit	**costume** (m)	[kɔstym]
dress (frock)	**robe** (f)	[rɔb]
skirt (garment)	**jupe** (f)	[ʒyp]
blouse	**chemisette** (f)	[ʃəmizɛt]
knitted jacket	**gilet** (m) **en laine**	[ʒilɛ ɑ̃ lɛn]
jacket (of woman's suit)	**jaquette** (f)	[ʒakɛt]
shawl	**foulard** (m)	[fular]
T-shirt	**tee-shirt** (m)	[tiʃœrt]
shorts (short trousers)	**short** (m)	[ʃɔrt]
tracksuit	**costume** (m) **de sport**	[kɔstym də spɔr]
bathrobe	**robe** (f) **de chambre**	[rɔb də ʃɑ̃br]
pajamas	**pyjama** (m)	[piʒama]
sweater	**chandail** (m)	[ʃɑ̃daj]
pullover	**pull** (m)	[pyl]
vest	**gilet** (m)	[ʒilɛ]
tailcoat	**queue-de-pie** (f)	[kødpi]
tuxedo	**smoking** (m)	[smɔkiŋ]

uniform	**uniforme** (f)	[ynifɔrm]
workwear	**tenue** (f) **de travail**	[təny də travaj]
overalls	**salopette** (f)	[salɔpɛt]
coat (e.g., doctor's ~)	**blouse** (f)	[bluz]

34. Clothing. Underwear

underwear	**sous-vêtements** (m pl)	[suvɛtmɑ̃]
undershirt (underwear)	**maillot** (m) **de corps**	[majo də kɔr]
socks	**chaussettes** (f pl)	[ʃosɛt]
nightgown	**chemise** (f) **de nuit**	[ʃəmiz də nɥi]
bra	**soutien-gorge** (m)	[sutjɛ̃gɔrʒ]
knee highs	**chaussettes** (f pl) **hautes**	[ʃosɛt ot]
pantyhose	**collant** (m)	[kɔlɑ̃]
stockings	**bas** (m pl)	[ba]
bathing suit	**maillot** (m) **de bain**	[majo də bɛ̃]

35. Headwear

hat	**bonnet** (m)	[bɔnɛ]
fedora	**chapeau** (m)	[ʃapo]
baseball cap	**casquette** (f) **de base-ball**	[kaskɛt də bɛzbol]
cap	**casquette** (f)	[kaskɛt]
beret	**béret** (m)	[berɛ]
hood	**capuche** (f)	[kapyʃ]
panama	**panama** (m)	[panama]
knitted hat	**bonnet** (m) **de laine**	[bɔnɛ də lɛn]
headscarf	**foulard** (m)	[fular]
women's hat	**chapeau** (m)	[ʃapo]
scarf (headscarf)	**fichu** (m)	[fiʃy]
hard hat	**casque** (m)	[kask]
garrison cap	**calot** (m)	[kalo]
helmet	**casque** (m)	[kask]
derby	**melon** (m)	[məlɔ̃]
top hat	**haut** (m) **de forme**	[o də fɔrm]

36. Footwear

footwear	**chaussures** (f pl)	[ʃosyr]
ankle boots	**bottines** (f pl)	[bɔtin]
shoes (wingtip shoes)	**souliers** (m pl)	[sulje]

boots (e.g., cowboy ~)	**bottes** (m pl)	[bɔt]
slippers	**chaussons** (m pl)	[ʃosõ]
tennis shoes	**baskets** (m pl)	[baskɛt]
sneakers	**tennis** (m pl)	[tenis]
sandals	**sandales** (f pl)	[sãdal]
cobbler	**cordonnier** (m)	[kɔrdɔnje]
heel (of shoe)	**talon** (m)	[talõ]
pair (of shoes)	**paire** (f)	[pɛr]
shoestring	**lacet** (m)	[lase]
to lace (vt)	**lacer**	[lase]
shoehorn	**chausse-pied** (m)	[ʃospje]
shoe polish	**cirage** (m)	[siraʒ]

37. Personal accessories

gloves	**gants** (m pl)	[gã]
mittens	**moufles** (f pl)	[mufl]
scarf (long)	**écharpe** (f)	[eʃarp]
glasses	**lunettes** (f pl)	[lynɛt]
frame (for spectacles)	**monture** (f)	[mõtyr]
umbrella	**parapluie** (m)	[paraplɥi]
walking stick	**canne** (f)	[kan]
hairbrush	**brosse** (f) **à cheveux**	[brɔs ɑ ʃəvø]
fan (accessory)	**éventail** (m)	[evãtaj]
necktie	**cravate** (f)	[kravat]
bow tie	**nœud papillon** (m)	[nø papijõ]
suspenders	**bretelles** (f pl)	[brətɛl]
handkerchief	**mouchoir** (m)	[muʃwar]
comb (for hair)	**peigne** (m)	[pɛɲ]
barrette	**barrette** (f)	[barɛt]
hairpin	**épingle** (f) **à cheveux**	[epɛ̃gl ɑ ʃəvø]
buckle	**boucle** (f)	[bukl]
belt	**ceinture** (f)	[sɛ̃tyr]
strap	**bandoulière** (f)	[bãduljɛr]
bag	**sac** (m)	[sak]
purse	**sac** (m) **à main**	[sak ɑ mɛ̃]
backpack	**sac** (m) **à dos**	[sak ɑ do]

38. Clothing. Miscellaneous

fashion	**mode** (f)	[mɔd]
in vogue	**à la mode**	[ɑlamɔd]

fashion designer	**couturier** (m)	[kutyrje]
collar	**col** (m)	[kɔl]
pocket	**poche** (f)	[pɔʃ]
pocket (e.g., ~ camera)	**de poche**	[də pɔʃ]
sleeve	**manche** (f)	[mɑ̃ʃ]
tab (loop)	**bride** (f)	[brid]
fly (on trousers)	**braguette** (f)	[bragɛt]
zipper (fastener)	**fermeture** (f) **à glissière**	[fɛrmətyr ɑ glisjɛr]
fastener	**agrafe** (f)	[agraf]
button	**bouton** (m)	[butɔ̃]
buttonhole	**boutonnière** (f)	[butɔnjɛr]
to come off (ab. button)	**s'arracher**	[saraʃe]
to sew (vi, vt)	**coudre**	[kudr]
to embroider (vi, vt)	**broder**	[brɔde]
embroidery	**broderie** (f)	[brɔdri]
sewing needle	**aiguille** (f)	[egɥij]
thread	**fil** (m)	[fil]
seam	**couture** (f)	[kutyr]
to get dirty (vi)	**se salir**	[sə salir]
stain (mark, spot)	**tâche** (f)	[taʃ]
to get creased (vi)	**se froisser**	[sə frwase]
to tear (vt)	**déchirer**	[deʃire]
clothes moth	**mite** (f)	[mit]

39. Personal care. Cosmetics

toothpaste	**dentifrice** (m)	[dɑ̃tifris]
toothbrush	**brosse** (f) **à dents**	[brɔs ɑ dɑ̃]
to brush one's teeth	**se brosser les dents**	[sə brɔse le dɑ̃]
razor	**rasoir** (m)	[razwar]
shaving cream	**crème** (f) **à raser**	[krɛm ɑ raze]
to shave (vi)	**se raser**	[sə raze]
soap	**savon** (m)	[savɔ̃]
shampoo	**shampooing** (m)	[ʃɑ̃pwɛ̃]
scissors	**ciseaux** (m pl)	[sizo]
nail file	**lime** (f) **à ongles**	[lim ɑ ɔ̃gl]
nail clippers	**pinces** (f pl) **à ongles**	[pɛ̃s ɑ ɔ̃gl]
tweezers	**pince** (f)	[pɛ̃s]
cosmetics	**produits** (m pl) **de beauté**	[prɔdyi də bote]
face mask	**masque** (m)	[mask]
manicure	**manucure** (f)	[manykyr]
to have a manicure	**se faire les ongles**	[sə fɛr le zɔ̃gl]
pedicure	**pédicure** (f)	[pedikyr]

beautician	esthéticien (m), -ne (f)	[ɛstetisjɛ̃, -ɛn]
make-up bag	trousse (f) de toilette	[trus də twalɛt]
powder (for face)	poudre (f)	[pudr]
powder compact	poudrier (m)	[pudrije]
blusher	fard (m) à joues	[far ɑ ʒu]
perfume (bottled)	parfum (m)	[parfœ̃]
toilet water	eau (f) de toilette	[o də twalɛt]
lotion	lotion (f)	[losjɔ̃]
cologne	eau de Cologne (f)	[o də kɔlɔŋ]
eyeshadow	fard (m) à paupières	[far ɑ popjɛr]
eyeliner	crayon (m) à paupières	[krɛjɔ̃ ɑ popjɛr]
mascara	mascara (m)	[maskara]
lipstick	rouge (m) à lèvres	[ruʒ ɑ lɛvr]
nail polish, enamel	vernis (m) à ongles	[vɛrni ɑ ɔ̃gl]
hair spray	laque (f) pour les cheveux	[lak pur le ʃəvø]
deodorant	déodorant (m)	[deɔdɔrɑ̃]
cream	crème (f)	[krɛm]
face cream	crème (f) pour le visage	[krɛm pur lə vizaʒ]
hand cream	crème (f) pour les mains	[krɛm pur le mɛ̃]
wrinkle cream	crème (f) anti-rides	[krɛm ɑ̃tirid]
day (attr)	de jour	[də ʒur]
night (attr)	de nuit	[də nɥi]
tampon	tampon (m)	[tɑ̃pɔ̃]
toilet paper	papier (m) de toilette	[papje də twalɛt]
hair dryer	sèche-cheveux (m)	[sɛʃʃəvø]

40. Watches. Clocks

watch	montre (f)	[mɔ̃tr]
dial	cadran (m)	[kadrɑ̃]
hand (of clock, watch)	aiguille (f)	[egɥij]
bracelet	bracelet (m)	[braslɛ]
watch strap	bracelet (m)	[braslɛ]
battery	pile (f)	[pil]
to be dead (battery)	se décharger	[sə deʃarʒe]
to change a battery	changer de pile	[ʃɑ̃ʒe də pil]
to run fast	avancer	[avɑ̃se]
to run slow	retarder	[rətarde]
wall clock	pendule (f)	[pɑ̃dyl]
hourglass	sablier (m)	[sablije]
sundial	cadran (m) solaire	[kadrɑ̃ sɔlɛr]
alarm clock	réveil (m)	[revɛj]

watchmaker	**horloger** (m)	[ɔrlɔʒe]
to repair (vt)	**réparer**	[repare]

EVERYDAY EXPERIENCE

41. Money

money	**argent** (m)	[arʒɑ̃]
exchange	**échange** (m)	[eʃɑ̃ʒ]
exchange rate	**cours** (m) **de change**	[kur də ʃɑ̃ʒ]
ATM	**distributeur** (m)	[distribytœr]
coin	**monnaie** (f)	[mɔnɛ]
dollar	**dollar** (m)	[dɔlar]
euro	**euro** (m)	[øro]
lira (currency)	**lire** (f)	[lir]
Deutschmark	**marque** (f)	[mark]
franc	**franc** (m)	[frɑ̃]
pound sterling	**livre** (f)	[livr]
yen	**yen** (m)	[jɛn]
debt	**dette** (f)	[dɛt]
debtor	**débiteur** (m)	[debitœr]
to lend (money)	**prêter**	[prete]
to borrow (vi, vt)	**emprunter**	[ɑ̃prœ̃te]
bank	**banque** (f)	[bɑ̃k]
account	**compte** (m)	[kɔ̃t]
to make a deposit	**verser sur le compte**	[vɛrse syr lə kɔ̃t]
to withdraw (vt)	**retirer du compte**	[rətire dy kɔ̃t]
credit card	**carte** (f) **de crédit**	[kart də kredi]
cash	**espèces** (f pl)	[ɛspɛs]
check	**chèque** (m)	[ʃɛk]
to write a check	**faire un chèque**	[fɛr œ̃ ʃɛk]
checkbook	**chéquier** (m)	[ʃekje]
wallet	**portefeuille** (m)	[pɔrtəfœj]
change purse	**bourse** (f)	[burs]
safe	**coffre fort** (m)	[kɔfr fɔr]
heir	**héritier** (m)	[eritje]
inheritance	**héritage** (m)	[eritaʒ]
fortune (wealth)	**fortune** (f)	[fɔrtyn]
lease, rent	**location** (f)	[lɔkasjɔ̃]
rent money	**loyer** (m)	[lwaje]
to rent (of a tenant)	**louer**	[lwe]

price	**prix** (m)	[pri]
cost	**coût** (m)	[ku]
sum (amount of money)	**somme** (f)	[sɔm]

to spend (vi, vt)	**dépenser**	[depɑ̃se]
expenses	**dépenses** (f pl)	[depɑ̃s]
to economize (vi, vt)	**économiser**	[ekɔnɔmize]
economical	**économe**	[ekɔnɔm]

to pay (vi, vt)	**payer**	[peje]
payment	**paiement** (m)	[pɛmɑ̃]
change (give the ~)	**monnaie** (f)	[mɔnɛ]

tax	**impôt** (m)	[ɛ̃po]
fine	**amende** (f)	[amɑ̃d]
to fine	**mettre qn à l´amende**	[mɛtr ... ɑ lamɑ̃d]

42. Post. Postal service

post office	**poste** (f)	[pɔst]
mail (letters etc.)	**courrier** (m)	[kurje]
mailman	**facteur** (m)	[faktœr]
working hours	**heures** (pl) **d'ouverture**	[zœr duvɛrtyr]

letter	**lettre** (f)	[lɛtr]
registered letter	**recommandé** (m)	[rəkɔmɑ̃de]
postcard	**carte** (f) **postale**	[kart pɔstal]
telegram	**télégramme** (m)	[telegram]
parcel	**colis** (m)	[kɔli]
money transfer	**mandat** (m) **postal**	[mɑ̃da pɔstal]

to receive (vt)	**recevoir**	[rəsəvwar]
to send (vt)	**envoyer**	[ɑ̃vwaje]
sending	**envoi** (m)	[ɑ̃vwa]

address	**adresse** (f)	[adrɛs]
ZIP code	**code** (m) **postal**	[kɔd pɔstal]
addressee	**destinataire** (m)	[dɛstinatɛr]
sender	**expéditeur** (m)	[ɛkspeditœr]
recipient (of letter)	**destinataire** (m)	[dɛstinatɛr]

name	**prénom** (m)	[prenɔ̃]
family name	**nom** (m) **de famille**	[nɔ̃ də famij]
Attn …	**à l'attention de …**	[alatɑ̃sjɔ̃ də]

rate (of postage)	**tarif** (m)	[tarif]
ordinary	**normal**	[nɔrmal]
economic	**économique**	[ekɔnɔmik]
weight	**poids** (m)	[pwa]
to weigh (in the balance)	**peser**	[pəze]

envelope	**enveloppe** (f)	[ãvlɔp]
postage stamp	**timbre** (m)	[tɛ̃br]

43. Banking

bank	**banque** (f)	[bɑ̃k]
branch (of bank etc.)	**agence** (f)	[aʒɑ̃s]
consultant	**conseiller** (m)	[kɔ̃seje]
manager (boss)	**gérant** (m)	[ʒerɑ̃]
banking account	**compte** (m)	[kɔ̃t]
account number	**numéro** (m) **du compte**	[nymero dy kɔ̃t]
checking account	**compte** (m) **courant**	[kɔ̃t kurɑ̃]
savings account	**compte** (m) **sur livret**	[kɔ̃t syr livrɛ]
to open an account	**ouvrir un compte**	[uvrir œ̃ kɔ̃t]
to close the account	**clôturer le compte**	[klotyre lə kɔ̃t]
to deposit (vt)	**verser sur le compte**	[vɛrse syr lə kɔ̃t]
to withdraw (vt)	**retirer du compte**	[rətire dy kɔ̃t]
deposit	**dépôt** (m)	[depo]
to make a deposit	**faire un dépôt**	[fɛr œ̃ depo]
transfer	**transfert** (m)	[trɑ̃sfɛr]
to transfer (money)	**réaliser un transfert**	[realize œ̃ trɑ̃sfɛr]
sum (amount of money)	**somme** (f)	[sɔm]
How much?	**Combien?**	[kɔ̃bjɛ̃]
signature	**signature** (f)	[siɲatyr]
to sign (vt)	**signer**	[siɲe]
credit card	**carte** (f) **de crédit**	[kart də kredi]
code	**code** (m)	[kɔd]
credit card number	**numéro** (m) **de carte de crédit**	[nymero də kart də kredi]
ATM	**distributeur** (m)	[distribytœr]
check	**chèque** (m)	[ʃɛk]
to write a check	**faire un chèque**	[fɛr œ̃ ʃɛk]
checkbook	**chéquier** (m)	[ʃekje]
credit (loan)	**crédit** (m)	[kredi]
to apply for credit	**demander un crédit**	[dəmɑ̃de œ̃ kredi]
to be given credit	**prendre un crédit**	[prɑ̃dr œ̃ kredi]
to grant a credit	**accorder un crédit**	[akɔrde œ̃ kredi]
guarantee	**gage** (m)	[gaʒ]

44. Telephone. Phone conversation

telephone	**téléphone** (m)	[telefɔn]
mobile phone	**portable** (m)	[pɔrtabl]
answering machine	**répondeur** (m)	[repɔ̃dœr]
to call (telephone)	**téléphoner, appeler**	[telefɔne], [aple]
phone call	**appel** (m)	[apɛl]
to dial a number	**composer le numéro**	[kɔ̃poze lə nymero]
Hello!	**Allô!**	[alo]
to ask (vi, vt)	**demander**	[dəmɑ̃de]
to answer (vi, vt)	**répondre**	[repɔ̃dr]
to hear (vi, vt)	**entendre**	[ɑ̃tɑ̃dr]
well	**bien**	[bjɛ̃]
not good, bad (adv)	**mal**	[mal]
noises	**bruits** (m pl)	[brɥi]
receiver	**récepteur** (m)	[resɛptœr]
busy	**occupé**	[ɔkype]
to ring (about phone)	**sonner**	[sɔ̃e]
telephone book	**carnet** (m) **de téléphone**	[karnɛ də telefɔn]
local	**local**	[lɔkal]
long distance (e.g., ~ call)	**interurbain**	[ɛ̃tɛryrbɛ̃]
international	**international**	[ɛ̃tɛrnasjɔnal]

45. Mobile telephone

mobile phone	**portable** (m)	[pɔrtabl]
display	**écran** (m)	[ekrɑ̃]
button	**bouton** (m)	[butɔ̃]
SIM card	**carte SIM** (f)	[kart sɪm]
battery	**pile** (f)	[pil]
to be dead (battery)	**être déchargé**	[ɛtr deʃarʒe]
charger	**chargeur** (m)	[ʃarʒœr]
menu	**carte** (f)	[kart]
settings	**réglages** (m pl)	[reglaʒ]
tune (melody)	**mélodie** (f)	[melɔdi]
to choose (select)	**choisir**	[ʃwazir]
calculator	**calculatrice** (f)	[kalkylatris]
answering machine	**répondeur** (m)	[repɔ̃dœr]
alarm clock	**réveil** (m)	[revɛj]
contacts	**liste** (f) **de contacts**	[list də kɔ̃takt]
SMS (text message)	**SMS** (m)	[esemes]
subscriber	**abonné** (m)	[abɔne]

46. Stationery

pen	**stylo** (m)	[stilo]
ballpoint pen	**stylo** (m) **à bille**	[stilo a bij]
fountain pen	**stylo** (m) **à plume**	[stilo a plym]
pencil	**crayon** (m)	[krɛjõ]
highlighter	**marqueur** (m)	[markœr]
felt-tip pen	**feutre** (m)	[føtr]
notepad	**bloc-notes** (m)	[blɔknɔt]
datebook	**agenda** (m)	[aʒɛ̃da]
ruler	**règle** (f)	[rɛgl]
calculator	**calculatrice** (f)	[kalkylatris]
eraser	**gomme** (f)	[gɔm]
thumbtack	**punaise** (f)	[pynɛz]
paper clip	**trombone** (m)	[trõbɔn]
glue	**colle** (f)	[kɔl]
stapler	**agrafeuse** (f)	[agraføz]
punch	**perforateur** (m)	[pɛrfɔratœr]
pencil sharpener	**taille-crayon** (m)	[tajkrɛjõ]
pointer	**pointeur** (m), **baguette** (f)	[pwɛ̃tœr], [bagɛt]
card index	**cartothèque** (f)	[kartɔtɛk]
label	**étiquette** (f)	[etikɛt]

47. Foreign languages

language	**langue** (f)	[lãg]
foreign language	**langue** (f) **étrangère**	[lãg etrãʒɛr]
to study (vt)	**étudier**	[etydje]
to learn (language etc.)	**apprendre**	[aprãdr]
to read (vi, vt)	**lire**	[lir]
to speak (vi, vt)	**parler**	[parle]
to understand (vt)	**comprendre**	[kõprãdr]
to write (vi, vt)	**écrire**	[ekrir]
fast	**vite**	[vit]
slowly	**lentement**	[lãtmã]
fluently	**couramment**	[kuramã]
rules	**règles** (f pl)	[rɛgl]
grammar	**grammaire** (f)	[gramɛr]
vocabulary	**lexique** (m)	[lɛksik]
phonetics	**phonétique** (f)	[fɔnetik]
textbook	**manuel** (m)	[manɥɛl]

dictionary	**dictionnaire** (m)	[diksjɔnɛr]
teach-yourself book	**manuel** (m) **autodidacte**	[manɥɛl otodidakt]
phrasebook	**guide** (m) **de conversation**	[gid də kɔ̃vɛrsasjɔ̃]
cassette	**cassette** (f)	[kasɛt]
videotape	**cassette** (f) **vidéo**	[kasɛt video]
CD (compact disc)	**disque CD** (m)	[disk sede]
DVD	**DVD** (m)	[devede]
alphabet	**alphabet** (m)	[alfabɛ]
to spell (vt)	**épeler**	[eple]
pronunciation	**prononciation** (f)	[prɔnɔ̃sjasjɔ̃]
accent	**accent** (m)	[aksɑ̃]
with an accent	**avec un accent**	[avɛk œn aksɑ̃]
without an accent	**sans accent**	[sɑ̃ zaksɑ̃]
word	**mot** (m)	[mo]
meaning	**sens** (m)	[sɑ̃s]
course (e.g., a French ~)	**cours** (m pl)	[kur]
to sign up	**s'inscrire**	[sɛ̃skrir]
teacher	**professeur** (m)	[prɔfɛsœr]
translation (process)	**traduction** (f)	[tradyksjɔ̃]
translation (text etc.)	**traduction** (f)	[tradyksjɔ̃]
translator	**traducteur** (m)	[tradyktœr]
interpreter	**interprète** (m)	[ɛ̃tɛrprɛt]
polyglot	**polyglotte** (m)	[pɔliglɔt]
memory	**mémoire** (f)	[memwar]

MEALS. RESTAURANT

48. Table setting

spoon	**cuiller** (f)	[kɥijɛr]
knife	**couteau** (m)	[kuto]
fork	**fourchette** (f)	[furʃɛt]
cup (of coffee)	**tasse** (f)	[tɑs]
dinner plate	**assiette** (f)	[asjɛt]
saucer	**soucoupe** (f)	[sukup]
napkin (on table)	**serviette** (f)	[sɛrvjɛt]
toothpick	**cure-dent** (f)	[kyrdã]

49. Restaurant

restaurant	**restaurant** (m)	[rɛstɔrã]
café	**café** (m)	[kafe]
coffee house	**café** (m)	[kafe]
pub, bar	**bar** (m)	[bar]
tearoom	**salon** (m) **de thé**	[salɔ̃ də te]
waiter	**serveur** (m)	[sɛrvœr]
waitress	**serveuse** (f)	[sɛrvøz]
bartender	**barman** (m)	[barman]
menu	**carte** (f)	[kart]
wine list	**carte** (f) **des vins**	[kart de vɛ̃]
to book a table	**réserver une table**	[rezɛrve yn tabl]
course, dish	**plat** (m)	[pla]
to order (meal)	**commander**	[kɔmãde]
to make an order	**faire la commande**	[fɛr la kɔmãd]
aperitif	**apéritif** (m)	[aperitif]
appetizer	**hors-d'œuvre** (m)	[ɔrdœvr]
dessert	**dessert** (m)	[desɛr]
check	**addition** (f)	[adisjɔ̃]
to pay the check	**régler l'addition**	[regle ladisjɔ̃]
to give change	**rendre la monnaie**	[rãdr la mɔnɛ]
tip	**pourboire** (m)	[purbwar]

50. Meals

food (noun)	nourriture (f)	[nurityr]
to eat (vi, vt)	manger	[mɑ̃ʒe]
breakfast	petit déjeuner (m)	[pəti deʒœne]
to have breakfast	prendre le petit déjeuner	[prɑ̃dr ləpti deʒœne]
lunch	déjeuner (m)	[deʒœne]
to have lunch	déjeuner	[deʒœne]
dinner (evening meal)	dîner (m)	[dine]
to have dinner	dîner	[dine]
appetite	appétit (m)	[apeti]
Enjoy your meal!	Bon appétit!	[bɔn apeti]
to open (e.g., ~ a bottle)	ouvrir	[uvrir]
to spill (liquid)	renverser	[rɑ̃vɛrse]
to spill out (vi)	se renverser	[sə rɑ̃vɛrse]
to boil (vi)	bouillir	[bujir]
to boil (vt)	faire bouillir	[fɛr bujir]
boiled	bouilli	[buji]
to cool (vt)	refroidir	[rəfrwadir]
to cool down (vi)	se refroidir	[sə rəfrwadir]
taste, flavor	goût (m)	[gu]
aftertaste	arrière-goût (m)	[arjɛrgu]
to be on a diet	suivre un régime	[sɥivr œ̃ reʒim]
diet	régime (m)	[reʒim]
vitamin	vitamine (f)	[vitamin]
calorie	calorie (f)	[kalɔri]
vegetarian (noun)	végétarien (m)	[veʒetarjɛ̃]
vegetarian (adj)	végétarien	[veʒetarjɛ̃]
fats (nutrient)	lipides (m pl)	[lipid]
proteins	protéines (f pl)	[prɔtein]
carbohydrates	glucides (m pl)	[glysid]
slice (of lemon, ham)	tranche (f)	[trɑ̃ʃ]
piece (of cake, pie)	morceau (m)	[mɔrso]
crumb (of bread)	miette (f)	[mjɛt]

51. Cooked dishes

course, dish	plat (m)	[pla]
cuisine	cuisine (f)	[kɥizin]
recipe	recette (f)	[rəsɛt]
portion	portion (f)	[pɔrsjɔ̃]

salad	**salade** (f)	[salad]
beet salad	**salade** (f) **russe**	[salad rys]
soup	**soupe** (f)	[sup]
clear soup (broth)	**bouillon** (m)	[bujɔ̃]
sandwich (bread)	**sandwich** (m)	[sɑ̃dwitʃ]
fried eggs	**les œufs brouillés**	[lezø bruje]
cutlet	**boulette** (f)	[bulɛt]
hamburger (beefburger)	**hamburger** (m)	[ɑ̃bœrgœr]
beefsteak	**steak** (m)	[stɛk]
roast meat	**rôti** (m)	[roti]
side dish	**garniture** (f)	[garnityr]
spaghetti	**spaghettis** (m pl)	[spagɛti]
mashed potatoes	**purée** (f)	[pyre]
pizza	**pizza** (f)	[pidza]
oatmeal (porridge)	**bouillie** (f)	[buji]
omelet	**omelette** (f)	[ɔmlɛt]
boiled (e.g., ~ beef)	**cuit à l'eau**	[kɥitɑlo]
smoked	**fumé**	[fyme]
fried	**frit**	[fri]
dried	**sec**	[sɛk]
frozen	**congelé**	[kɔ̃ʒle]
pickled	**mariné**	[marine]
sweet (in taste)	**sucré**	[sykre]
salty	**salé**	[sale]
cold	**froid**	[frwa]
hot	**chaud**	[ʃo]
bitter	**amer**	[amɛr]
tasty	**bon**	[bɔ̃]
to cook (vt)	**cuire à l'eau**	[kɥir ɑ lo]
to cook (vi)	**préparer**	[prepare]
to fry (vt)	**faire frire**	[fɛr frir]
to heat up (food)	**réchauffer**	[reʃofe]
to salt (vt)	**saler**	[sale]
to pepper (vt)	**poivrer**	[pwavre]
to grate (vt)	**râper**	[rɑpe]
peel (noun)	**peau** (f)	[po]
to peel (vt)	**éplucher**	[eplyʃe]

52. Food

meat	**viande** (f)	[vjɑ̃d]
chicken	**poulet** (m)	[pulɛ]
young chicken	**poulet** (m)	[pulɛ]

duck	**canard** (m)	[kanar]
goose	**oie** (f)	[wa]
game	**gibier** (m)	[ʒibje]
turkey	**dinde** (f)	[dɛ̃d]
pork	**du porc**	[dy pɔr]
veal	**du veau**	[dy vo]
lamb	**du mouton**	[dy mutɔ̃]
beef	**du bœuf**	[dy bœf]
rabbit	**lapin** (m)	[lapɛ̃]
sausage (salami etc.)	**saucisson** (m)	[sosisɔ̃]
hot dog (frankfurter)	**saucisse** (f)	[sosis]
bacon	**bacon** (m)	[bekɔn]
ham	**jambon** (m)	[ʒãbɔ̃]
gammon	**cuisse** (f)	[kɥis]
pâté	**pâté** (m)	[pɑte]
liver	**foie** (m)	[fwa]
lard	**lard** (m)	[lar]
ground beef	**farce** (f)	[fars]
tongue	**langue** (f)	[lãg]
egg	**œuf** (m)	[œf]
eggs	**les œufs**	[lezø]
egg white	**blanc** (m) **d'œuf**	[blã dœf]
egg yolk	**jaune** (m) **d'œuf**	[ʒon dœf]
fish	**poisson** (m)	[pwasɔ̃]
seafood	**produits** (m pl) **de mer**	[prɔdyi də mɛr]
caviar	**caviar** (m)	[kavjar]
crab	**crabe** (m)	[krab]
shrimp	**crevette** (f)	[krəvɛt]
oyster	**huître** (f)	[ɥitr]
spiny lobster	**langoustine** (f)	[lãgustin]
octopus	**poulpe** (m)	[pulp]
squid	**calamar** (m)	[kalamar]
sturgeon	**esturgeon** (m)	[ɛstyrʒɔ̃]
salmon	**saumon** (m)	[somɔ̃]
halibut	**flétan** (m)	[fletã]
cod	**morue** (f)	[mɔry]
mackerel	**maquereau** (m)	[makro]
tuna	**thon** (m)	[tɔ̃]
eel	**anguille** (f)	[ãgij]
trout	**truite** (f)	[trɥit]
sardine	**sardine** (f)	[sardin]
pike	**brochet** (m)	[brɔʃɛ]
herring	**hareng** (m)	[arã]

bread	pain (m)	[pɛ̃]
cheese	fromage (m)	[frɔmaʒ]
sugar	sucre (m)	[sykr]
salt	sel (m)	[sɛl]

rice	riz (m)	[ri]
pasta	pâtes (m pl)	[pɑt]
noodles	nouilles (f pl)	[nuj]

butter	beurre (m)	[bœr]
oil	huile (f)	[ɥil]
sunflower oil	l'huile de tournesol	[lɥil də turnəsɔl]
margarine	margarine (f)	[margarin]

| olives | olives (f pl) | [ɔliv] |
| olive oil | l'huile d'olive | [lɥil dɔliv] |

milk	lait (m)	[lɛ]
condensed milk	lait (m) condensé	[lɛ kɔ̃dɑ̃se]
yogurt	yogourt (m)	[jaurt]
sour cream	crème (f) fraîche	[krɛm frɛʃ]
cream (of milk)	crème (f)	[krɛm]

| mayonnaise | sauce (f) mayonnaise | [sos majɔnɛz] |
| cream (filling for biscuits) | crème (f) | [krɛm] |

cereal grains	gruau (m)	[gryo]
flour	farine (f)	[farin]
canned food	conserves (f pl)	[kɔ̃sɛrv]

cornflakes	pop-corn (m)	[pɔpkɔrn]
honey	miel (m)	[mjɛl]
jelly (e.g., strawberry ~)	marmelade (f)	[marmələad]
chewing gum	gomme (f) à mâcher	[gɔm ɑ mɑʃe]

53. Drinks

water	eau (f)	[o]
drinking water	l'eau potable	[lo pɔtabl]
mineral water	l'eau minérale	[lo mineral]

still	plate	[plat]
carbonated	gazeuse	[gazøz]
sparkling	gazeuse	[gazøz]
ice	glace (f)	[glas]
with ice	avec de la glace	[avɛk dəla glas]

| non-alcoholic | sans alcool | [sɑ̃ zalkɔl] |
| soft drink | boisson (f) non alcoolisée | [bwasɔ̃ nonalkɔlize] |

cool soft drink	**rafraîchissement** (m)	[rafrɛʃismɑ̃]
lemonade	**limonade** (f)	[limɔnad]
liquor	**boissons** (f pl) **alcoolisées**	[bwasɔ̃ alkɔlize]
wine	**vin** (m)	[vɛ̃]
white wine	**vin** (m) **blanc**	[vɛ̃ blɑ̃]
red wine	**vin** (m) **rouge**	[vɛ̃ ruʒ]
liqueur	**liqueur** (f)	[likœr]
champagne	**champagne** (m)	[ʃɑ̃paɲ]
vermouth	**vermouth** (m)	[vɛrmut]
whisky	**whisky** (m)	[wiski]
vodka	**vodka** (f)	[vɔdka]
gin	**gin** (m)	[dʒin]
cognac	**cognac** (m)	[kɔɲak]
rum	**rhum** (m)	[rɔm]
coffee	**café** (m)	[kafe]
black coffee	**café** (m) **noir**	[kafe nwar]
coffee with milk	**café** (m) **au lait**	[kafe o lɛ]
cappuccino	**café** (m) **crème**	[kafe krɛm]
instant coffee	**café** (m) **soluble**	[kafe sɔlybl]
milk	**lait** (m)	[lɛ]
cocktail	**cocktail** (m)	[kɔktɛl]
milk shake	**cocktail** (m) **au lait**	[kɔktɛl o lɛ]
juice	**jus** (m)	[ʒy]
tomato juice	**jus** (m) **de tomate**	[ʒy də tɔmat]
orange juice	**jus** (m) **d´orange**	[ʒy dɔrɑ̃ʒ]
freshly squeezed juice	**jus** (m) **pressé**	[ʒy prese]
beer	**bière** (f)	[bjɛr]
light beer	**bière** (f) **blonde**	[bjɛr blɔ̃d]
dark beer	**bière** (f) **brune**	[bjɛr bryn]
tea	**thé** (m)	[te]
black tea	**thé** (m) **noir**	[te nwar]
green tea	**thé** (m) **vert**	[te vɛr]

54. Vegetables

vegetables	**légumes** (m pl)	[legym]
greens	**verdure** (f)	[vɛrdyr]
tomato	**tomate** (f)	[tɔmat]
cucumber	**concombre** (m)	[kɔ̃kɔ̃br]
carrot	**carotte** (f)	[karɔt]

potato	pomme (f) de terre	[pɔm də tɛr]
onion	oignon (m)	[ɔɲɔ̃]
garlic	ail (m)	[aj]

cabbage	chou (m)	[ʃu]
cauliflower	chou-fleur (m)	[ʃuflœr]
Brussels sprouts	chou (m) de Bruxelles	[ʃu də brysɛl]
broccoli	brocoli (m)	[brɔkɔli]

beet	betterave (f)	[bɛtrav]
eggplant	aubergine (f)	[obɛrʒin]
zucchini	courgette (f)	[kurʒɛt]
pumpkin	potiron (m)	[pɔtirɔ̃]
turnip	navet (m)	[navɛ]

parsley	persil (m)	[pɛrsi]
dill	fenouil (m)	[fənuj]
lettuce	salade (f)	[salad]
celery	céleri (m)	[sɛlri]
asparagus	asperge (f)	[aspɛrʒ]
spinach	épinard (m)	[epinar]

pea	pois (m)	[pwa]
beans	fèves (m pl)	[fɛv]
corn (maize)	maïs (m)	[mais]
kidney bean	haricot (m)	[ariko]

bell pepper	poivre (m)	[pwavr]
radish	radis (m)	[radi]
artichoke	artichaut (m)	[artiʃo]

55. Fruits. Nuts

fruit	fruit (m)	[frɥi]
apple	pomme (f)	[pɔm]
pear	poire (f)	[pwar]
lemon	citron (m)	[sitrɔ̃]
orange	orange (f)	[ɔrɑ̃ʒ]
strawberry	fraise (f)	[frɛz]

mandarin	mandarine (f)	[mɑ̃darin]
plum	prune (f)	[pryn]
peach	pêche (f)	[pɛʃ]
apricot	abricot (m)	[abriko]
raspberry	framboise (f)	[frɑ̃bwaz]
pineapple	ananas (m)	[anana]

banana	banane (f)	[banan]
watermelon	pastèque (f)	[pastɛk]
grapes	raisin (m)	[rɛzɛ̃]

cherry (sour cherry)	**cerise** (f)	[səriz]
cherry (sweet cherry)	**cerise** (f)	[səriz]
melon	**melon** (m)	[məlɔ̃]

grapefruit	**pamplemousse** (m)	[pɑ̃pləmus]
avocado	**avocat** (m)	[avɔka]
papaya	**papaye** (f)	[papaj]
mango	**mangue** (f)	[mɑ̃g]
pomegranate	**grenade** (f)	[grənad]

redcurrant	**groseille** (f) **rouge**	[grozɛj ruʒ]
blackcurrant	**cassis** (m)	[kasis]
gooseberry	**groseille** (f) **verte**	[grozɛj vɛrt]
bilberry	**myrtille** (f)	[mirtij]
blackberry	**mûre** (f)	[myr]

raisin	**raisin** (m) **sec**	[rɛzɛ̃ sɛk]
fig	**figue** (f)	[fig]
date	**datte** (f)	[dat]

peanut	**cacahuète** (f)	[kakawɛt]
almond	**amande** (f)	[amɑ̃d]
walnut	**noix** (f)	[nwa]
hazelnut	**noisette** (f)	[nwazɛt]
coconut	**noix** (f) **de coco**	[nwa də kɔkɔ]
pistachios	**pistaches** (f pl)	[pistaʃ]

56. Bread. Candy

| confectionery (pastry) | **confiserie** (f) | [kɔ̃fizri] |
| bread | **pain** (m) | [pɛ̃] |

| small roll (bread) | **brioche** (f) | [brijɔʃ] |
| cookies | **biscuit** (m) | [biskɥi] |

chocolate (noun)	**chocolat** (m)	[ʃɔkɔla]
chocolate (attr)	**en chocolat**	[ɑ̃ ʃɔkɔla]
candy	**bonbon** (m)	[bɔ̃bɔ̃]

| cake (e.g., cupcake) | **gâteau** (m) | [gato] |
| cake (e.g., birthday ~) | **tarte** (f) | [tart] |

| pie (e.g., apple ~) | **gâteau** (m) | [gato] |
| filling (for cake, pie) | **garniture** (f) | [garnityr] |

| jam | **confiture** (f) | [kɔ̃fityr] |
| marmalade | **marmelade** (f) | [marmǝlad] |

| wafer | **gaufre** (f) | [gofr] |
| ice-cream | **glace** (f) | [glas] |

57. Spices

salt	**sel** (m)	[sɛl]
salty	**salé**	[sale]
to salt (vt)	**saler**	[sale]
black pepper	**poivre** (m) **noir**	[pwavr nwar]
red pepper	**poivre** (m) **rouge**	[pwavr ruʒ]
mustard	**moutarde** (f)	[mutard]
horseradish	**raifort** (m)	[rɛfɔr]
seasoning (condiment)	**condiment** (m)	[kɔ̃dimɑ̃]
spice	**épice** (f)	[epis]
sauce	**sauce** (f)	[sos]
vinegar	**vinaigre** (m)	[vinɛgr]
anise	**anis** (m)	[ani(s)]
basil	**basilic** (m)	[bazilik]
cloves	**clou** (m) **de girofle**	[klu də ʒirɔfl]
ginger	**gingembre** (m)	[ʒɛ̃ʒɑ̃br]
coriander	**coriandre** (m)	[kɔrjɑ̃dr]
cinnamon	**cannelle** (f)	[kanɛl]
sesame	**sésame** (m)	[sezam]
bay leaf	**feuille** (f) **de laurier**	[fœj də lɔrje]
paprika	**paprika** (m)	[paprika]
caraway	**cumin** (m)	[kymɛ̃]
saffron	**safran** (m)	[safrɑ̃]

PERSONAL INFORMATION. FAMILY

58. Personal information. Forms

name, first name	**prénom** (m)	[prenɔ̃]
family name	**nom** (m) **de famille**	[nɔ̃ də famij]
date of birth	**date** (f) **de naissance**	[dat də nɛsɑ̃s]
place of birth	**né à …**	[ne a]
nationality	**nationalité** (f)	[nasjɔnalite]
place of residence	**domicile** (m)	[dɔmisil]
country	**pays** (m)	[pei]
profession (occupation)	**profession** (f)	[prɔfɛsjɔ̃]
gender, sex	**sexe** (m)	[sɛks]
height	**taille** (f)	[taj]
weight	**poids** (m)	[pwa]

59. Family members. Relatives

mother	**mère** (f)	[mɛr]
father	**père** (m)	[pɛr]
son	**fils** (m)	[fis]
daughter	**fille** (f)	[fij]
younger daughter	**fille** (f) **cadette**	[fij kadɛt]
younger son	**fils** (m) **cadet**	[fis kadɛ]
elder daughter	**fille** (f) **aînée**	[fij ene]
elder son	**fils** (m) **aîné**	[fis ene]
brother	**frère** (m)	[frɛr]
sister	**sœur** (f)	[sœr]
cousin (masc.)	**cousin** (m)	[kuzɛ̃]
cousin (fem.)	**cousine** (f)	[kuzin]
mom	**maman** (f)	[mamɑ̃]
dad, daddy	**papa** (m)	[papa]
parents	**parents** (pl)	[parɑ̃]
child (boy or girl)	**enfant** (m, f)	[ɑ̃fɑ̃]
children	**enfants** (pl)	[ɑ̃fɑ̃]
grandmother	**grand-mère** (f)	[grɑ̃mɛr]
grandfather	**grand-père** (m)	[grɑ̃pɛr]
grandson	**petit-fils** (m)	[pti fis]
granddaughter	**petite-fille** (f)	[ptit fij]

grandchildren	**petits-enfants** (pl)	[pətizɑ̃fɑ̃]
uncle	**oncle** (m)	[ɔ̃kl]
aunt	**tante** (f)	[tɑ̃t]
nephew	**neveu** (m)	[nəvø]
niece	**nièce** (f)	[njɛs]
mother-in-law	**belle-mère** (f)	[bɛlmɛr]
father-in-law	**beau-père** (m)	[bopɛr]
son-in-law	**gendre** (m)	[ʒɑ̃dr]
stepmother	**belle-mère, marâtre** (f)	[bɛlmɛr], [marɑtr]
stepfather	**beau-père** (m)	[bopɛr]
baby (infant)	**bébé** (m)	[bebe]
infant	**bébé** (m)	[bebe]
little boy, kid	**petit** (m)	[pti]
wife	**femme** (f)	[fam]
husband	**mari** (m)	[mari]
spouse (husband)	**époux** (m)	[epu]
spouse (wife)	**épouse** (f)	[epuz]
married (man)	**marié**	[marje]
married (woman)	**mariée**	[marje]
single (unmarried)	**célibataire**	[selibatɛr]
bachelor	**célibataire** (m)	[selibatɛr]
divorced (man)	**divorcé**	[divɔrse]
widow	**veuve** (f)	[vœv]
widower	**veuf** (m)	[vœf]
relative	**parent** (m)	[parɑ̃]
close relative	**parent** (m) **proche**	[parɑ̃ prɔʃ]
distant relative	**parent** (m) **éloigné**	[parɑ̃ elwaɲe]
relatives	**parents** (m pl)	[parɑ̃]
orphan (boy or girl)	**orphelin** (m)	[ɔrfəlɛ̃]
guardian (of minor)	**tuteur** (m)	[tytœr]
to adopt (a boy)	**adopter**	[adɔpte]
to adopt (a girl)	**adopter**	[adɔpte]

60. Friends. Coworkers

friend (man)	**ami** (m)	[ami]
friend (girlfriend)	**amie** (f)	[ami]
friendship	**amitié** (f)	[amitje]
to be friends	**être ami**	[ɛtr ami]
buddy (man)	**copain** (m)	[kɔpɛ̃]
buddy (woman)	**copine** (f)	[kɔpin]
comrade (politics)	**camarade** (m)	[kamarad]
partner	**partenaire** (m)	[partənɛr]

business partner	**partenaire** (m) **d´affaire**	[partənɛr dafɛr]
chief (boss)	**chef** (m)	[ʃɛf]
boss, superior	**supérieur** (m)	[syperjœr]
subordinate	**subordonné** (m)	[sybɔrdɔne]
colleague	**collègue** (m, f)	[kɔlɛg]
acquaintance (person)	**connaissance** (f)	[kɔnɛsɑ̃s]
traveling companion	**compagnon** (m) **de route**	[kɔ̃paɲɔ̃ də rut]
classmate	**copain** (m) **de classe**	[kɔpɛ̃ də klas]
neighbor (man)	**voisin** (m)	[vwazɛ̃]
neighbor (woman)	**voisine** (f)	[vwazin]
neighbors	**voisins** (pl)	[vwazɛ̃]

HUMAN BODY. MEDICINE

61. Head

head	**tête** (f)	[tɛt]
face	**visage** (m)	[vizaʒ]
nose	**nez** (m)	[ne]
mouth	**bouche** (f)	[buʃ]
eye	**œil** (m)	[œj]
eyes	**les yeux**	[lezjø]
pupil	**pupille** (f)	[pypij]
eyebrow	**sourcil** (m)	[sursi]
eyelash	**cil** (m)	[sil]
eyelid	**paupière** (f)	[popjɛr]
tongue	**langue** (f)	[lɑ̃g]
tooth	**dent** (f)	[dɑ̃]
lips	**lèvres** (f pl)	[lɛvr]
cheekbones	**pommettes** (f pl)	[pɔmɛt]
gum	**gencive** (f)	[ʒɑ̃siv]
palate	**palais** (m)	[palɛ]
nostrils	**narines** (f pl)	[narin]
chin	**menton** (m)	[mɑ̃tɔ̃]
jaw	**mâchoire** (f)	[mɑʃwar]
cheek	**joue** (f)	[ʒu]
forehead	**front** (m)	[frɔ̃]
temple	**tempe** (f)	[tɑ̃p]
ear	**oreille** (f)	[ɔrɛj]
back of the head	**nuque** (f)	[nyk]
neck	**cou** (m)	[ku]
throat	**gorge** (f)	[gɔrʒ]
hair	**cheveux** (m pl)	[ʃəvø]
hairstyle	**coiffure** (f)	[kwafyr]
haircut	**coupe** (f)	[kup]
wig	**perruque** (f)	[peryk]
mustache	**moustache** (f)	[mustaʃ]
beard	**barbe** (f)	[barb]
to have (a beard etc.)	**porter**	[pɔrte]
braid	**tresse** (f)	[trɛs]
sideburns	**favoris** (m pl)	[favɔri]
red-haired	**roux**	[ru]

gray (hair)	**gris**	[gri]
bald	**chauve**	[ʃov]
bald patch	**calvitie** (f)	[kalvisi]

| ponytail | **queue** (f) **de cheval** | [kø də ʃəval] |
| bangs | **frange** (f) | [frɑ̃ʒ] |

62. Human body

| hand | **main** (f) | [mɛ̃] |
| arm | **bras** (m) | [bra] |

finger, toe	**doigt** (m)	[dwa]
thumb	**pouce** (m)	[pus]
little finger	**petit doigt** (m)	[pəti dwa]
nail	**ongle** (m)	[ɔ̃gl]

fist	**poing** (m)	[pwɛ̃]
palm	**paume** (f)	[pom]
wrist	**poignet** (m)	[pwaɲɛ]
forearm	**avant-bras** (m)	[avɑ̃bra]
elbow	**coude** (m)	[kud]
shoulder	**épaule** (f)	[epol]

leg	**jambe** (f)	[ʒɑ̃b]
foot	**pied** (m)	[pje]
knee	**genou** (m)	[ʒənu]
calf (part of leg)	**mollet** (m)	[mɔlɛ]

| hip | **hanche** (f) | [ɑ̃ʃ] |
| heel | **talon** (m) | [talɔ̃] |

body	**corps** (m)	[kɔr]
stomach (abdomen)	**ventre** (m)	[vɑ̃tr]
chest	**poitrine** (f)	[pwatrin]
breast	**sein** (m)	[sɛ̃]
side (of the body)	**côté** (m)	[kote]
back	**dos** (m)	[do]

| lower back | **reins** (m pl) | [rɛ̃] |
| waist | **taille** (f) | [taj] |

navel	**nombril** (m)	[nɔ̃bril]
buttocks	**fesses** (f pl)	[fɛs]
behind	**derrière** (m)	[dɛrjɛr]

beauty mark	**grain** (m) **de beauté**	[grɛ̃ də bote]
birthmark	**envie** (f)	[ɑ̃vi]
tattoo	**tatouage** (m)	[tatwaʒ]
scar	**cicatrice** (f)	[sikatris]

63. Diseases

sickness	**maladie** (f)	[maladi]
to be sick	**être malade**	[ɛtr malad]
health	**santé** (f)	[sɑ̃te]
runny nose	**rhume** (m)	[rym]
tonsillitis	**angine** (f)	[ɑ̃ʒin]
cold	**refroidissement** (m)	[rəfrwadismɑ̃]
to catch a cold	**attraper un rhume**	[atrape œ̃ rym]
bronchitis	**bronchite** (f)	[brɔ̃ʃit]
pneumonia	**pneumonie** (f)	[pnømɔni]
flu, influenza	**grippe** (f)	[grip]
near-sighted	**myope**	[mjɔp]
far-sighted	**presbyte**	[prɛsbit]
strabismus	**strabisme** (m)	[strabism]
cross-eyed	**strabique**	[strabik]
cataract	**cataracte** (f)	[katarakt]
glaucoma	**glaucome** (m)	[glokom]
stroke	**hémorragie** (f) **cérébrale**	[emɔraʒi serebral]
heart attack	**infarctus** (m)	[ɛ̃farktys]
myocardial infarction	**infarctus** (m) **de myocarde**	[ɛ̃farktys də mjɔkard]
paralysis	**paralysie** (f)	[paralizi]
to paralyze (vt)	**paralyser**	[paralize]
allergy	**allergie** (f)	[alɛrʒi]
asthma	**asthme** (m)	[asm]
diabetes	**diabète** (f)	[djabɛt]
toothache	**mal** (m) **de dents**	[mal də dɑ̃]
caries	**carie** (f)	[kari]
diarrhea	**diarrhée** (f)	[djare]
constipation	**constipation** (f)	[kɔ̃stipasjɔ̃]
stomach upset	**diarrhée** (f)	[djare]
food poisoning	**empoisonnement** (m)	[ɑ̃pwazɔnmɑ̃]
arthritis	**arthrite** (f)	[artrit]
rickets	**rachitisme** (m)	[raʃitism]
rheumatism	**rhumatisme** (m)	[rymatism]
atherosclerosis	**athérosclérose** (f)	[ateroskleroz]
gastritis	**gastrite** (f)	[gastrit]
appendicitis	**appendicite** (f)	[apɛ̃disit]
cholecystitis	**cholécystite** (f)	[kɔlesistit]
ulcer	**ulcère** (m)	[ylsɛr]
measles	**rougeole** (f)	[ruʒɔl]

German measles	**roséole** (f)	[rozeɔl]
jaundice	**jaunisse** (f)	[ʒonis]
hepatitis	**hépatite** (f)	[epatit]
schizophrenia	**schizophrénie** (f)	[skizɔfreni]
hydrophobia, rabies	**rage** (f)	[raʒ]
neurosis	**névrose** (m)	[nevroz]
concussion	**commotion** (f) **du cerveau**	[kɔmɔsjɔ̃ dy sɛrvo]
cancer	**cancer** (m)	[kɑ̃sɛr]
sclerosis	**sclérose** (f)	[skleroz]
multiple sclerosis	**sclérose** (f) **en plaques**	[skleroz ɑ̃ plak]
alcoholism	**alcoolisme** (m)	[alkɔlism]
alcoholic (noun)	**alcoolique** (m)	[alkɔlik]
syphilis	**syphilis** (f)	[sifilis]
AIDS	**SIDA** (m)	[sida]
tumor	**tumeur** (f)	[tymœr]
malignant	**maligne**	[maliɲ]
benign	**bénigne**	[beniɲ]
fever	**fièvre** (f)	[fjɛvr]
malaria	**paludisme** (m)	[palydism]
gangrene	**gangrène** (f)	[gɑ̃grɛn]
seasickness	**mal** (m) **de mer**	[mal də mɛr]
epilepsy	**épilepsie** (f)	[epilɛpsi]
epidemic	**épidémie** (f)	[epidemi]
typhus	**typhus** (m)	[tifys]
tuberculosis	**tuberculose** (f)	[tybɛrkyloz]
cholera	**choléra** (m)	[kɔlera]
plague (bubonic ~)	**peste** (f)	[pɛst]

64. Symptoms. Treatments. Part 1

symptom	**symptôme** (m)	[sɛ̃ptom]
temperature	**température** (f)	[tɑ̃peratyr]
high temperature	**fièvre** (f)	[fjɛvr]
pulse	**pouls** (m)	[pu]
giddiness	**vertige** (m)	[vɛrtiʒ]
hot	**chaud**	[ʃo]
shivering	**frisson** (m)	[frisɔ̃]
pale (e.g., ~ face)	**pâle**	[pɑl]
cough	**toux** (f)	[tu]
to cough (vi)	**tousser**	[tuse]
to sneeze (vi)	**éternuer**	[etɛrnɥe]

faint	**évanouissement** (m)	[evanwismɑ̃]
to faint (vi)	**s'évanouir**	[sevanwir]
bruise	**bleu** (m)	[blø]
bump (lump)	**bosse** (f)	[bɔs]
to bruise oneself	**se heurter**	[sə œrte]
bruise	**meurtrissure** (f)	[mœrtrisyr]
to get bruised	**se faire mal**	[sə fɛr mal]
to limp (vi)	**boiter**	[bwate]
dislocation	**foulure** (f)	[fulyr]
to dislocate (vt)	**se démettre**	[sə demɛtr]
fracture	**fracture** (f)	[fraktyr]
to get a fracture	**avoir une fracture**	[avwar yn fraktyr]
cut (e.g., on the finger)	**coupure** (f)	[kupyr]
to cut oneself	**se couper**	[sə kupe]
bleeding	**hémorragie** (f)	[emɔraʒi]
burn (injury)	**brûlure** (f)	[brylyr]
to burn oneself	**se brûler**	[sə bryle]
to prick (vt)	**se piquer**	[sə pike]
to prick oneself	**se piquer**	[sə pike]
to injure (vt)	**blesser**	[blese]
injury	**blessure** (f)	[blesyr]
wound	**blessure** (f)	[blesyr]
trauma	**trauma** (m)	[troma]
to be delirious	**délirer**	[delire]
to stutter (vi)	**bégayer**	[begeje]
sunstroke	**coup** (m) **de soleil**	[ku də sɔlɛj]

65. Symptoms. Treatments. Part 2

pain (physical)	**douleur** (f)	[dulœr]
splinter (in foot, finger)	**écharde** (f)	[eʃard]
sweat (perspiration)	**sueur** (f)	[sɥœr]
to sweat (perspire)	**suer**	[sɥe]
vomiting	**vomissement** (m)	[vɔmismɑ̃]
convulsions	**spasmes** (m pl)	[spasm]
pregnant	**enceinte**	[ɑ̃sɛ̃t]
to be born	**naître**	[nɛtr]
delivery, labor	**accouchement** (m)	[akuʃmɑ̃]
to be in labor	**accoucher**	[akuʃe]
abortion	**avortement** (m)	[avɔrtəmɑ̃]
respiration	**respiration** (f)	[rɛspirasjɔ̃]
inhalation	**inhalation** (f)	[inalasjɔ̃]

exhalation	expiration (f)	[ɛkspirasjɔ̃]
to breathe out	expirer	[ɛkspire]
to breathe in	inhaler	[inale]

disabled person	invalide (m)	[ɛ̃valid]
cripple	handicapé (m)	[ɑ̃dikape]
drug addict	drogué (m)	[drɔge]

deaf	sourd	[sur]
dumb	muet	[mɥɛ]
deaf-and-dumb	sourd-muet	[surmɥɛ]

madman	fou (m)	[fu]
madwoman	folle (f)	[fɔl]
to go insane	devenir fou	[dəvnir fu]

gene	gène (m)	[ʒɛn]
immunity	immunité (f)	[imynite]
hereditary	héréditaire	[ereditɛr]
congenital	congénital	[kɔ̃ʒenital]

virus	virus (m)	[virys]
microbe	microbe (m)	[mikrɔb]
bacterium	bactérie (f)	[bakteri]
infection	infection (f)	[ɛ̃fɛksjɔ̃]

66. Symptoms. Treatments. Part 3

| hospital | hôpital (m) | [ɔpital] |
| patient | patient (m) | [pasjɑ̃] |

diagnosis	diagnostic (m)	[djagnɔstik]
cure, treatment	traitement (m)	[trɛtmɑ̃]
treatment	traitement (m)	[trɛtmɑ̃]
to get treatment	se faire soigner	[sə fɛr swaɲe]
to treat (vt)	traiter (vt)	[trete]
to nurse (vt)	soigner	[swaɲe]
care (treatment)	soin (m)	[swɛ̃]

operation, surgery	opération (f)	[ɔperasjɔ̃]
to bandage (head, limb)	panser	[pɑ̃se]
bandaging	pansement (m)	[pɑ̃smɑ̃]

vaccination	vaccination (f)	[vaksinasjɔ̃]
to vaccinate (vt)	vacciner	[vaksine]
injection, shot	piqûre (f)	[pikyr]
to give an injection	faire une piqûre	[fɛr yn pikyr]

| amputation | amputation (f) | [ɑ̃pytasjɔ̃] |
| to amputate (vt) | amputer | [ɑ̃pyte] |

coma	**coma** (m)	[kɔma]
to be in a coma	**être dans le coma**	[ɛtr dã lə kɔma]
intensive care	**réanimation** (f)	[reanimasjɔ̃]
to recover (~ from flu)	**se rétablir**	[sə retablir]
state (patient's ~)	**état** (m)	[eta]
consciousness	**conscience** (f)	[kɔ̃sjãs]
memory (faculty)	**mémoire** (f)	[memwar]
to extract (tooth)	**arracher**	[araʃe]
filling (in tooth)	**plombage** (m)	[plɔ̃baʒ]
to fill (vt)	**plomber**	[plɔ̃be]
hypnosis	**hypnose** (f)	[ipnoz]
to hypnotize (vt)	**hypnotiser**	[ipnɔtize]

67. Medicine. Drugs. Accessories

medicine, drug	**médicament** (m)	[medikamã]
remedy	**remède** (m)	[rəmɛd]
prescription	**ordonnance** (f)	[ɔrdɔnãs]
tablet, pill	**comprimé** (m)	[kɔ̃prime]
ointment	**onguent** (m)	[ɔ̃gã]
ampule	**ampoule** (f)	[ãpul]
mixture	**mixture** (f)	[mikstyr]
syrup	**sirop** (m)	[siro]
pill	**pilule** (f)	[pilyl]
powder	**poudre** (f)	[pudr]
bandage	**bande** (f)	[bãd]
cotton wool	**coton** (m)	[kɔtɔ̃]
iodine	**iode** (m)	[jɔd]
Band-Aid	**sparadrap** (m)	[sparadra]
eyedropper	**compte-gouttes** (f)	[kɔ̃tgut]
thermometer	**thermomètre** (m)	[tɛrmɔmɛtr]
syringe	**seringue** (f)	[sərɛ̃g]
wheelchair	**fauteuil** (m) **roulant**	[fotœj rulã]
crutches	**béquilles** (f pl)	[bekij]
painkiller	**anesthésique** (m)	[anɛstezik]
laxative	**purgatif** (m)	[pyrgatif]
spirit	**alcool** (m)	[alkɔl]
medicinal herbs	**herbe** (f) **médicinale**	[ɛrb medisinal]
herbal	**d'herbes**	[dɛrb]

APARTMENT

68. Apartment

apartment	**appartement** (m)	[apartəmɑ̃]
room	**chambre** (f)	[ʃɑ̃br]
bedroom	**chambre** (f) **à coucher**	[ʃɑ̃br ɑ kuʃe]
dining room	**salle** (f) **à manger**	[sal ɑ mɑ̃ʒe]
living room	**salon** (m)	[salɔ̃]
study	**cabinet** (m)	[kabinɛ]
entrance hall	**antichambre** (f)	[ɑ̃tiʃɑ̃br]
bathroom	**salle** (f) **de bains**	[sal də bɛ̃]
half bath	**toilettes** (f pl)	[twalɛt]
ceiling	**plafond** (m)	[plafɔ̃]
floor	**plancher** (m)	[plɑ̃ʃe]
corner (inside room)	**coin** (m)	[kwɛ̃]

69. Furniture. Interior

furniture (for house)	**meuble** (m)	[mœbl]
table	**table** (f)	[tabl]
chair	**chaise** (f)	[ʃɛz]
bed	**lit** (m)	[li]
couch, sofa	**canapé** (m)	[kanape]
armchair	**fauteuil** (m)	[fotœj]
bookcase	**bibliothèque** (f)	[biblijɔtɛk]
shelf	**rayon** (m)	[rɛjɔ̃]
set of shelves	**étagère** (f)	[etaʒɛr]
wardrobe	**armoire** (f)	[armwar]
coat rack	**patère** (f)	[patɛr]
coat stand	**portemanteau** (m)	[pɔrtmɑ̃to]
chest of drawers	**commode** (f)	[kɔmɔd]
coffee table	**table** (f) **basse**	[tabl bas]
mirror	**miroir** (m), **glace** (f)	[mirwar], [glas]
carpet	**tapis** (m)	[tapi]
rug, small carpet	**petit tapis** (m)	[pəti tapi]
fireplace	**cheminée** (f)	[ʃəmine]
candle	**bougie** (f)	[buʒi]

candlestick	chandelier (m)	[ʃɑ̃dəlje]
kitchen curtains	rideaux (m pl) de cuisine	[rido də kɥizin]
drapes	rideaux (m pl)	[rido]
wallpaper	papier (m) peint	[papje pɛ̃]
blinds (jalousie)	jalousies (f pl)	[ʒaluzi]
table lamp	lampe (f)	[lɑ̃p]
floor lamp	lampadaire (m)	[lɑ̃padɛr]
chandelier	lustre (m)	[lystr]
leg (of chair, table)	pied (m)	[pje]
arm (of chair)	accoudoir (m)	[akudwar]
back	dossier (m)	[dosje]
drawer	tiroir (m)	[tirwar]

70. Bedding

bedclothes	linge (m)	[lɛ̃ʒ]
pillow	oreiller (m)	[ɔrɛje]
pillowcase	taie (f) d'oreiller	[tɛ dɔrɛje]
blanket (comforter)	couverture (f)	[kuvɛrtyr]
sheet	drap (m)	[dra]
bedspread	couvre-lit (m)	[kuvrəli]

71. Kitchen

kitchen	cuisine (f)	[kɥizin]
gas	gaz (m)	[gaz]
gas stove	cuisinière (f) à gaz	[kɥizinjɛr a gaz]
electric stove	cuisinière (f) électrique	[kɥizinjɛr elɛktrik]
oven	four (m)	[fur]
microwave oven	four (m) micro-ondes	[fur mikrɔɔ̃d]
fridge	réfrigérateur (m)	[refriʒeratœr]
freezer	congélateur (m)	[kɔ̃ʒelatœr]
dishwasher	lave-vaisselle (m)	[lavvesɛl]
meat grinder	hachoir (m)	[aʃwar]
juicer	presse-agrumes (m)	[prɛsagrym]
toaster	grille-pain (m)	[grijpɛ̃]
mixer	batteur (m)	[batœr]
coffee maker	machine (f) à café	[maʃin a kafe]
coffee pot	cafetière (f)	[kaftjɛr]
coffee grinder	moulin (m) à café	[mulɛ̃ a kafe]
kettle	bouilloire (f)	[bujwar]
teapot	théière (f)	[tejɛr]

lid	**couvercle** (m)	[kuvɛrkl]
tea strainer	**passe-thé** (f)	[pɑste]
spoon	**cuillère** (f)	[kɥijɛr]
teaspoon	**petite cuillère** (f)	[pətit kɥijɛr]
tablespoon	**cuillère** (f) **à soupe**	[kɥijɛr ɑ sup]
fork	**fourchette** (f)	[furʃɛt]
knife	**couteau** (m)	[kuto]
tableware	**vaisselle** (f)	[vɛsɛl]
plate	**assiette** (f)	[asjɛt]
saucer	**soucoupe** (f)	[sukup]
wineglass	**verre** (m) **à vodka**	[vɛr ɑ vɔdka]
glass (e.g., ~ of water)	**verre** (m)	[vɛr]
cup	**tasse** (f)	[tɑs]
sugar bowl	**sucrier** (m)	[sykrije]
salt shaker	**salière** (f)	[saljɛr]
pepper shaker	**poivrière** (f)	[pwavrijɛr]
butter dish	**beurrier** (m)	[bœrje]
saucepan	**casserole** (f)	[kasrɔl]
frying pan	**poêle** (f)	[pwal]
ladle	**louche** (f)	[luʃ]
colander	**passoire** (f)	[pɑswar]
tray	**plateau** (m)	[plato]
bottle	**bouteille** (f)	[butɛj]
jar (glass)	**bocal** (m)	[bɔkal]
can	**boîte** (f) **en métal**	[bwat ɑ̃ metal]
bottle opener	**ouvre-bouteille** (m)	[uvrəbutɛj]
can opener	**ouvre-boîte** (m)	[uvrəbwat]
corkscrew	**tire-bouchon** (m)	[tirbuʃɔ̃]
filter	**filtre** (m)	[filtr]
to filter (vt)	**filtrer**	[filtre]
trash	**ordures** (f pl)	[ɔrdyr]
trash can	**poubelle** (f)	[pubɛl]

72. Bathroom

bathroom	**salle** (f) **de bains**	[sal də bɛ̃]
water	**eau** (f)	[o]
tap, faucet	**robinet** (m)	[rɔbinɛ]
hot water	**l'eau chaude**	[lo ʃod]
cold water	**l'eau froide**	[lo frwad]
toothpaste	**dentifrice** (m)	[dɑ̃tifris]
to brush one's teeth	**se brosser les dents**	[sə brɔse le dɑ̃]

toothbrush	**brosse** (f) **à dents**	[brɔs ɑ dɑ̃]
to shave (vi)	**se raser**	[sə raze]
shaving foam	**mousse** (f) **à raser**	[mus ɑ raze]
razor	**rasoir** (m)	[razwar]

to wash (clean)	**laver**	[lave]
to take a bath	**se laver**	[sə lave]
shower	**douche** (f)	[duʃ]
to take a shower	**prendre une douche**	[prɑ̃dr yn duʃ]

bathtub	**baignoire** (f)	[bɛɲwar]
toilet	**cuvette** (f)	[kyvɛt]
water heater	**chaudière** (f)	[ʃodjɛr]
sink	**lavabo** (m)	[lavabo]

| soap | **savon** (m) | [savɔ̃] |
| soap dish | **porte-savon** (m) | [pɔrtsavɔ̃] |

sponge	**éponge** (f)	[epɔ̃ʒ]
shampoo	**shampooing** (m)	[ʃɑ̃pwɛ̃]
towel	**serviette** (f)	[sɛrvjɛt]
bathrobe	**robe** (f) **de chambre**	[rɔb də ʃɑ̃br]

laundry (process)	**lessive** (f)	[lɛsiv]
washing machine	**machine** (f) **à laver**	[maʃin ɑ lave]
to do the laundry	**faire la lessive**	[fɛr la lɛsiv]
laundry detergent	**lessive** (f)	[lɛsiv]

73. Household appliances

TV set	**télé** (f)	[tele]
tape recorder	**magnétophone** (m)	[maɲetofɔn]
video, VCR	**magnétoscope** (m)	[maɲetɔskɔp]
radio	**radio** (f)	[radjo]
player (CD, MP3 etc.)	**lecteur** (m)	[lɛktœr]

video projector	**vidéoprojecteur** (m)	[videoprɔʒɛktœr]
home movie theater	**home cinéma** (m)	[həʊm sinema]
DVD player	**lecteur** (m) **DVD**	[lɛktœr devede]
amplifier	**amplificateur** (m)	[ɑ̃plifikatœr]
video game console	**console** (f) **de jeux**	[kɔ̃sɔl də ʒø]

video camera	**caméscope** (m)	[kameskɔp]
camera (photo)	**appareil** (m) **photo**	[aparɛj foto]
digital camera	**appareil** (m) **photo numérique**	[aparɛj foto nymerik]

vacuum cleaner	**aspirateur** (m)	[aspiratœr]
iron (e.g., steam ~)	**fer** (m) **à repasser**	[fɛr ɑ rəpase]
ironing board	**planche** (f) **à repasser**	[plɑ̃ʃ ɑ rəpase]

telephone	**téléphone** (m)	[telefɔn]
mobile phone	**portable** (m)	[pɔrtabl]
typewriter	**machine** (f) **à écrire**	[maʃin ɑ ekrir]
sewing machine	**machine** (f) **à coudre**	[maʃin ɑ kudr]
microphone	**micro** (m)	[mikro]
headphones	**écouteurs** (m pl)	[ekutœr]
remote control (TV)	**télécommande** (f)	[telekɔmãd]
compact disc, CD	**disque CD** (m)	[disk sede]
cassette	**cassette** (f)	[kasɛt]
record (disc)	**disque** (m)	[disk]

THE EARTH. WEATHER

74. Outer space

cosmos	**cosmos** (m)	[kɔsmos]
space (e.g., ~ flight)	**cosmique**	[kɔsmik]
outer space	**l'espace cosmique**	[lɛspas kɔsmik]
universe	**univers** (m)	[ynivɛr]
galaxy	**galaxie** (f)	[galaksi]
star	**étoile** (f)	[etwal]
constellation	**constellation** (f)	[kɔ̃stelasjɔ̃]
planet	**planète** (f)	[planɛt]
satellite	**satellite** (m)	[satelit]
meteorite	**météorite** (m)	[meteɔrit]
comet	**comète** (f)	[kɔmɛt]
asteroid	**astéroïde** (m)	[asterɔid]
orbit	**orbite** (f)	[ɔrbit]
to rotate (vi)	**tourner**	[turne]
atmosphere	**atmosphère** (f)	[atmɔsfɛr]
the Sun	**Soleil** (m)	[sɔlɛj]
solar system	**système** (m) **solaire**	[sistɛm sɔlɛr]
solar eclipse	**l´éclipse de soleil**	[leklips də sɔlɛj]
the Earth	**Terre** (f)	[tɛr]
the Moon	**Lune** (f)	[lyn]
Mars	**Mars** (m)	[mars]
Venus	**Vénus** (f)	[venys]
Jupiter	**Jupiter** (m)	[ʒypitɛr]
Saturn	**Saturne** (m)	[satyrn]
Mercury	**Mercure** (m)	[mɛrkyr]
Uranus	**Uranus** (m)	[yranys]
Neptune	**Neptune** (m)	[nɛptyn]
Pluto	**Pluton** (m)	[plytɔ̃]
Milky Way	**La Voie Lactée**	[la vwa lakte]
Great Bear	**La Grande Ours**	[la grɑ̃d urs]
Pole Star	**étoile** (f) **Polaire**	[etwal pɔlɛr]
Martian	**martien** (m)	[marsjɛ̃]
extraterrestrial	**extraterrestre** (m)	[ɛkstratɛrɛstr]

| alien | **extraterrestre** (m) | [εkstratεrεstr] |
| flying saucer | **soucoupe** (f) **volante** | [sukup vɔlãt] |

spaceship	**vaisseau** (m) **spatial**	[vεso spasjal]
space station	**station** (f) **orbitale**	[stasjõ ɔrbital]
blast-off	**lancement** (m)	[lãsmã]

engine	**moteur** (m)	[mɔtœr]
nozzle	**tuyère** (f)	[tyjεr]
fuel	**carburant** (m)	[karbyrã]

cockpit, flight deck	**cabine** (f)	[kabin]
antenna	**antenne** (f)	[ãtεn]
porthole	**hublot** (m)	[yblo]
solar battery	**batterie** (f) **solaire**	[batri sɔlεr]
spacesuit	**scaphandre** (m)	[skafãdr]

| weightlessness | **apesanteur** (f) | [apəzãtœr] |
| oxygen | **oxygène** (m) | [ɔksiʒεn] |

| docking (in space) | **arrimage** (m) | [arimaʒ] |
| to dock (vi, vt) | **s'arrimer à ...** | [sarime a] |

observatory	**observatoire** (m)	[ɔpsεrvatwar]
telescope	**télescope** (m)	[teleskɔp]
to observe (vt)	**observer**	[ɔpsεrve]
to explore (vt)	**explorer**	[εksplɔre]

75. The Earth

the Earth	**Terre** (f)	[tεr]
globe	**globe** (m) **terrestre**	[glɔb tεrεstr]
planet	**planète** (f)	[planεt]

atmosphere	**atmosphère** (f)	[atmɔsfεr]
geography	**géographie** (f)	[ʒeɔgrafi]
nature	**nature** (f)	[natyr]

globe (model of Earth)	**globe** (m) **terrestre**	[glɔb tεrεstr]
map	**carte** (f)	[kart]
atlas	**atlas** (m)	[atlas]

Europe	**Europe** (f)	[ørɔp]
Asia	**Asie** (f)	[azi]
Africa	**Afrique** (f)	[afrik]
Australia	**Australie** (f)	[ostrali]

America	**Amérique** (f)	[amerik]
North America	**Amérique** (f) **du Nord**	[amerik dy nɔr]
South America	**Amérique** (f) **du Sud**	[amerik dy syd]

| Antarctica | **Antarctide** (f) | [ɑ̃tarktid] |
| the Arctic | **Arctique** (f) | [arktik] |

76. Cardinal directions

north	**nord** (m)	[nɔr]
to the north	**vers le nord**	[vɛr lə nɔr]
in the north	**au nord**	[onɔr]
northern	**du nord**	[dy nɔr]

south	**sud** (m)	[syd]
to the south	**vers le sud**	[vɛr lə syd]
in the south	**au sud**	[osyd]
southern	**du sud**	[dy syd]

west	**occident** (m)	[ɔksidɑ̃]
to the west	**vers l'occident**	[vɛr lɔksidɑ̃]
in the west	**à l'occident**	[alɔksidɑ̃]
western	**occidental**	[ɔksidɑ̃tal]

east	**orient** (m)	[ɔrjɑ̃]
to the east	**vers l'orient**	[vɛr lɔrjɑ̃]
in the east	**à l'orient**	[alɔrjɑ̃]
eastern	**oriental**	[ɔrjɑ̃tal]

77. Sea. Ocean

sea	**mer** (f)	[mɛr]
ocean	**océan** (m)	[ɔseɑ̃]
gulf (bay)	**golfe** (m)	[gɔlf]
straits	**détroit** (m)	[detrwa]

| land | **terre** (f) | [tɛr] |
| continent (mainland) | **continent** (m) | [kɔ̃tinɑ̃] |

island	**île** (f)	[il]
peninsula	**presqu'île** (f)	[prɛskil]
archipelago	**archipel** (m)	[arʃipɛl]

bay	**baie** (f)	[bɛ]
harbor	**port** (m)	[pɔr]
lagoon	**lagune** (f)	[lagyn]
cape	**cap** (m)	[kap]

atoll	**atoll** (m)	[atɔl]
reef	**récif** (m)	[resif]
coral	**corail** (m)	[kɔraj]
coral reef	**récif** (m) **de corail**	[resif də kɔraj]

deep	**profond**	[prɔfɔ̃]
depth (deep water)	**profondeur** (f)	[prɔfɔ̃dœr]
abyss	**abîme** (m)	[abim]
trench (e.g., Mariana ~)	**fosse** (f) **océanique**	[fos ɔseanik]

| current | **courant** (m) | [kurã] |
| to surround (vt) | **baigner** | [beɲe] |

| shore | **côte** (f) | [kot] |
| coast | **littoral** (m) | [litɔral] |

high tide	**marée** (f) **haute**	[mare ot]
low tide	**marée** (f) **basse**	[mare bas]
sandbank	**banc** (m) **de sable**	[bã də sabl]
bottom	**fond** (m)	[fɔ̃]

wave	**vague** (f)	[vag]
crest (~ of a wave)	**crête** (f) **de l'onde**	[krɛt də lɔ̃d]
foam	**mousse** (f)	[mus]

hurricane	**ouragan** (m)	[uragã]
tsunami	**tsunami** (m)	[tsynami]
calm	**calme** (m)	[kalm]
quiet (e.g., ~ ocean)	**calme**	[kalm]

| pole | **pôle** (m) | [pol] |
| polar | **polaire** | [pɔlɛr] |

latitude	**latitude** (f)	[latityd]
longitude	**longitude** (f)	[lɔ̃ʒityd]
parallel	**parallèle** (f)	[paralɛl]
equator	**équateur** (m)	[ekwatœr]

sky	**ciel** (m)	[sjɛl]
horizon	**horizon** (m)	[ɔrizɔ̃]
air	**air** (m)	[ɛr]

lighthouse	**phare** (m)	[far]
to dive (vi)	**plonger**	[plɔ̃ʒe]
to sink (about boat)	**sombrer**	[sɔ̃bre]
treasures	**trésor** (m)	[trezɔr]

78. Seas' and Oceans' names

Atlantic Ocean	**océan** (m) **Atlantique**	[ɔsean atlãtik]
Indian Ocean	**océan** (m) **Indien**	[ɔsean ɛ̃djɛ̃]
Pacific Ocean	**océan** (m) **Pacifique**	[ɔseã pasifik]
Arctic Ocean	**océan** (m) **Glacial**	[ɔseã glasjal]
Black Sea	**mer** (f) **Noire**	[mɛr nwar]
Red Sea	**mer** (f) **Rouge**	[mɛr ruʒ]

Yellow Sea	mer (f) **Jaune**	[mɛr ʒon]
White Sea	mer (f) **Blanche**	[mɛr blɑ̃ʃ]
Caspian Sea	mer (f) **Caspienne**	[mɛr kaspjɛn]
Dead Sea	mer (f) **Morte**	[mɛr mɔrt]
Mediterranean Sea	mer (f) **Méditerranée**	[mɛr meditɛrane]
Aegean Sea	mer (f) **Égée**	[mɛr eʒe]
Adriatic Sea	mer (f) **Adriatique**	[mɛr adrijatik]
Arabian Sea	mer (f) **d´Oman**	[mɛr dɔman]
Sea of Japan	mer (f) **du Japon**	[mɛr dy ʒapɔ̃]
Bering Sea	mer (f) **de Béring**	[mɛr də beriŋ]
South China Sea	mer (f) **de Chine Méridionale**	[mɛr də ʃin meridjɔnal]
Coral Sea	mer (f) **de Corail**	[mɛr də kɔraj]
Tasman Sea	mer (f) **de Tasman**	[mɛr də tasman]
Caribbean Sea	mer (f) **Caraïbe**	[mɛr karaib]
Barents Sea	mer (f) **de Barents**	[mɛr də barɛ̃s]
Kara Sea	mer (f) **de Kara**	[mɛr də kara]
North Sea	mer (f) **du Nord**	[mɛr dy nɔr]
Baltic Sea	mer (f) **Baltique**	[mɛr baltik]
Norwegian Sea	mer (f) **de Norvège**	[mɛr də nɔrvɛʒ]

79. Mountains

mountain	**montagne** (f)	[mɔ̃taɲ]
mountain range	**chaîne** (f) **de montagnes**	[ʃɛn də mɔ̃taɲ]
mountain ridge	**crête** (f)	[krɛt]
summit, top	**sommet** (m)	[sɔmɛ]
peak	**pic** (m)	[pik]
foot (of mountain, hill)	**pied** (m)	[pje]
slope (mountainside)	**pente** (f)	[pɑ̃t]
volcano	**volcan** (m)	[vɔlkɑ̃]
active volcano	**volcan** (m) **actif**	[vɔlkɑn aktif]
dormant volcano	**volcan** (m) **éteint**	[vɔlkɑn etɛ̃]
eruption	**éruption** (f)	[erypsjɔ̃]
crater	**cratère** (m)	[kratɛr]
magma	**magma** (m)	[magma]
lava	**lave** (f)	[lav]
scorching	**incandescent**	[ɛ̃kɑ̃desɑ̃]
canyon	**canyon** (m)	[kanjɔ̃]
gorge	**défilé** (m)	[defile]

crevice	**crevasse** (f)	[krəvas]
pass, col	**col** (m)	[kɔl]
plateau	**plateau** (m)	[plato]
cliff	**rocher** (m)	[rɔʃe]
hill	**colline** (f)	[kɔlin]
glacier	**glacier** (m)	[glasje]
waterfall	**chute** (f) **d'eau**	[ʃyt do]
geyser	**geyser** (m)	[ʒɛzɛr]
lake	**lac** (m)	[lak]
plain	**plaine** (f)	[plɛn]
landscape	**paysage** (m)	[peizaʒ]
echo	**écho** (m)	[eko]
alpinist	**alpiniste** (m)	[alpinist]
rock climber	**varappeur** (m)	[varapœr]
conquer (in climbing)	**conquérir**	[kɔ̃kerir]
climb (e.g., an easy ~)	**ascension** (f)	[asɑ̃sjɔ̃]

80. Mountains names

Alps	**Alpes** (f pl)	[alp]
Mont Blanc	**Mont Blanc** (m)	[mɔ̃blɑ̃]
Pyrenees	**Pyrénées** (f pl)	[pirene]
Carpathians	**Carpates** (f pl)	[karpat]
Ural Mountains	**Monts Oural** (m pl)	[mɔ̃ ural]
Caucasus	**Caucase** (m)	[kokaz]
Elbrus	**Elbrous** (m)	[ɛlbrys]
Altai	**Altaï** (m)	[altaj]
Tien Shan	**Tian Chan** (m)	[tjɑ̃ ʃɑ̃]
Pamir Mountains	**Pamir** (m)	[pamir]
Himalayas	**Himalaya** (m)	[imalaja]
Everest	**Everest** (m)	[evrɛst]
Andes	**Andes** (f pl)	[ɑ̃d]
Cordilleras	**Cordillère** (f)	[kɔrdijɛr]
Kilimanjaro	**Kilimandjaro** (m)	[kilimɑ̃dʒaro]

81. Rivers

river	**rivière** (f), **fleuve** (m)	[rivjɛr], [flœv]
spring (natural source)	**source** (f)	[surs]
bed (of the river)	**lit** (m)	[li]
basin	**bassin** (m)	[basɛ̃]
to flow into ...	**se jeter dans ...**	[sə ʒəte dɑ̃]

tributary	**affluent** (m)	[aflyɑ̃]
bank (of river)	**rive** (f)	[riv]
current, stream	**courant** (m)	[kurɑ̃]
downstream	**en aval**	[ɑn aval]
upstream	**en amont**	[ɑn amɔ̃]
flood	**inondation** (f)	[inɔ̃dasjɔ̃]
flooding	**les grandes crues**	[le grɑ̃d kry]
to overflow (vi)	**déborder**	[debɔrde]
to flood (vt)	**inonder**	[inɔ̃de]
shallows	**bas-fond** (m)	[bafɔ̃]
rapids	**rapide** (m)	[rapid]
dam	**barrage** (m)	[baraʒ]
canal	**canal** (m)	[kanal]
reservoir, artificial lake	**retenue** (f) **d'eau**	[rətəny do]
sluice, lock	**écluse** (f)	[eklyz]
reservoir (water body)	**réservoir** (m) **d'eau**	[rezɛrvwar do]
marsh, swamp	**marais** (m)	[marɛ]
bog	**fondrière** (f)	[fɔ̃drijɛr]
whirlpool	**tourbillon** (m)	[turbijɔ̃]
stream (brook)	**ruisseau** (m)	[rɥiso]
drinking (about water)	**potable**	[pɔtabl]
fresh (not salt)	**doux**	[du]
ice	**glace** (f)	[glas]
to ice over	**être gelé**	[ɛtr ʒəle]

82. Rivers' names

Seine	**Seine** (f)	[sɛn]
Loire	**Loire** (f)	[lwar]
Thames	**Tamise** (f)	[tamiz]
Rhine	**Rhin** (m)	[rɛ̃]
Danube	**Danube** (m)	[danyb]
Volga	**Volga** (f)	[vɔlga]
Don	**Don** (m)	[dɔ̃]
Lena	**Lena** (f)	[lena]
Yellow River	**Huang He** (m)	[waŋ e]
Mekong	**Mékong** (m)	[mekɔ̃g]
Ganges	**Gange** (m)	[gɑ̃ʒ]
Nile River	**Nil** (m)	[nil]
Congo	**Congo** (m)	[kɔ̃go]

Okavango	**Okavango** (m)	[ɔkavangɔ]
Zambezi	**Zambèze** (m)	[zɑ̃bɛz]
Limpopo	**Limpopo** (m)	[limpɔpo]

83. Forest

forest	**forêt** (f)	[fɔrɛ]
forest (attr)	**forestier**	[fɔrɛstje]
thick forest	**fourré** (m)	[fure]
grove	**bosquet** (m)	[bɔskɛ]
clearing	**clairière** (f)	[klɛrjɛr]
thicket	**broussailles** (f pl)	[brusaj]
scrubland	**maquis** (m)	[maki]
pathway	**chemin** (m)	[ʃəmɛ̃]
footpath	**sentier** (m)	[sɑ̃tje]
gully	**ravin** (m)	[ravɛ̃]
tree	**arbre** (m)	[arbr]
leaf	**feuille** (f)	[fœj]
leaves	**feuillage** (m)	[fœjaʒ]
falling leaves	**chute** (f) **de feuilles**	[ʃyt də fœj]
to fall (about leaves)	**tomber**	[tɔ̃be]
top (of the tree)	**sommet** (m)	[sɔmɛ]
branch	**rameau** (m)	[ramo]
bough	**branche** (f)	[brɑ̃ʃ]
bud (on shrub, tree)	**bourgeon** (m)	[burʒɔ̃]
needle (of pine tree)	**aiguille** (f)	[eɡɥij]
cone (of pine, fir)	**pomme** (f) **de pin**	[pɔm də pɛ̃]
hollow (in a tree)	**creux** (m)	[krø]
nest	**nid** (m)	[ni]
burrow, animal hole	**trou** (m)	[tru]
trunk (of a tree)	**tronc** (m)	[trɔ̃]
root	**racine** (f)	[rasin]
bark (of a tree)	**écorce** (f)	[ekɔrs]
moss	**mousse** (f)	[mus]
to uproot (vt)	**déraciner** (vt)	[derasine]
to chop down	**abattre**	[abatr]
to deforest (vt)	**déboiser**	[debwaze]
tree stump	**souche** (f)	[suʃ]
campfire	**feu** (m) **de bois**	[fø də bwa]
forest fire	**incendie** (f)	[ɛ̃sɑ̃di]

to extinguish (vt)	**éteindre**	[etɛ̃dr]
forest ranger	**garde** (m) **forestier**	[gard fɔrɛstje]
protection	**protection** (f)	[prɔtɛksjɔ̃]
to protect (e.g., ~ nature)	**protéger**	[prɔteʒe]
poacher	**braconnier** (m)	[brakɔnje]
trap (e.g., bear ~)	**piège** (m) **à dents**	[pjɛʒ ɑ dɑ̃]
to gather, to pick (vt)	**cueillir**	[kœjir]
to lose one's way	**s'égarer**	[segare]

84. Natural resources

natural resources	**ressources** (f pl) **naturelles**	[rəsurs natyrɛl]
minerals	**minéraux** (m pl)	[minero]
deposit (e.g., coal ~)	**gisement** (m)	[ʒizmɑ̃]
field (e.g., oilfield)	**gisement** (m)	[ʒizmɑ̃]
to mine (extract)	**extraire**	[ɛkstrɛr]
mining (extraction)	**extraction** (f)	[ɛkstraksjɔ̃]
ore	**minerai** (m)	[minrɛ]
mine (e.g., for coal)	**mine** (f)	[min]
mineshaft, pit	**puits** (m) **de mine**	[pɥi də min]
miner	**mineur** (m)	[minœr]
gas	**gaz** (m)	[gaz]
gas pipeline	**gazoduc** (m)	[gazɔdyk]
oil (petroleum)	**pétrole** (m)	[petrɔl]
oil pipeline	**pipeline** (m)	[piplin]
oil rig	**derrick** (m)	[derik]
derrick	**tour** (f) **de forage**	[tur də fɔraʒ]
tanker	**pétrolier** (m)	[petrɔlje]
sand	**sable** (m)	[sabl]
limestone	**calcaire** (m)	[kalkɛr]
gravel	**gravier** (m)	[gravje]
peat	**tourbe** (f)	[turb]
clay	**argile** (f)	[arʒil]
coal	**charbon** (m)	[ʃarbɔ̃]
iron	**fer** (m)	[fɛr]
gold	**or** (m)	[ɔr]
silver	**argent** (m)	[arʒɑ̃]
nickel	**nickel** (m)	[nikɛl]
copper	**cuivre** (m)	[kɥivr]
zinc	**zinc** (m)	[zɛ̃g]
manganese	**manganèse** (m)	[mɑ̃ganɛz]
mercury	**mercure** (m)	[mɛrkyr]

lead	**plomb** (m)	[plɔ̃]
mineral	**minéral** (m)	[mineral]
crystal	**cristal** (m)	[kristal]
marble	**marbre** (m)	[marbr]
uranium	**uranium** (m)	[yranjɔm]
diamond (stone)	**diamant** (m)	[djamɑ̃]

85. Weather

weather	**temps** (m)	[tɑ̃]
weather forecast	**météo** (f)	[meteo]
temperature	**température** (f)	[tɑ̃peratyr]
thermometer	**thermomètre** (m)	[tɛrmɔmɛtr]
barometer	**baromètre** (m)	[barɔmɛtr]

humidity	**humidité** (f)	[ymidite]
heat (of summer)	**chaleur** (f)	[ʃalœr]
hot (torrid)	**très chaud**	[trɛ ʃo]
it's hot	**il fait très chaud**	[il fɛ trɛ ʃo]

| it's warm | **il fait chaud** | [il fɛʃo] |
| warm (moderately hot) | **chaud** | [ʃo] |

| it's cold | **il fait froid** | [il fɛ frwa] |
| cold | **froid** | [frwa] |

sun	**soleil** (m)	[sɔlɛj]
to shine	**briller**	[brije]
sunny (day)	**ensoleillé**	[ɑ̃sɔleje]
to come up (vi)	**se lever**	[sə ləve]
to set (vi)	**se coucher**	[sə kuʃe]

cloud	**nuage** (m)	[nɥaʒ]
cloudy	**nuageux**	[nɥaʒø]
rain cloud	**nuée** (f)	[nɥe]
somber (cloudy)	**sombre**	[sɔ̃br]

rain	**pluie** (f)	[plɥi]
it's raining	**il pleut**	[il plø]
rainy (day)	**pluvieux**	[plyvjø]
to drizzle (vi)	**bruiner**	[brɥine]

pouring rain	**pluie** (f) **torrentielle**	[plɥi tɔrɑ̃sjɛl]
downpour	**averse** (f)	[avɛrs]
heavy (e.g., ~ rain)	**forte**	[fɔrt]
puddle	**flaque** (f)	[flak]
to get wet (in rain)	**se faire mouiller**	[sə fɛr muje]

| mist (fog) | **brouillard** (m) | [brujar] |
| misty | **brumeux** | [brymø] |

| snow | **neige** (f) | [nɛʒ] |
| it's snowing | **il neige** | [il nɛʒ] |

86. Severe weather. Natural disasters

thunderstorm	**orage** (m)	[ɔraʒ]
lightning (~ strike)	**éclair** (m)	[eklɛr]
to flash (vi)	**éclater**	[eklate]

thunder	**tonnerre** (m)	[tɔnɛr]
to thunder (vi)	**gronder**	[grɔ̃de]
it's thundering	**le tonnerre gronde**	[lə tɔnɛr grɔ̃d]

| hail | **grêle** (f) | [grɛl] |
| it's hailing | **il grêle** | [il grɛl] |

| to flood (vt) | **inonder** | [inɔ̃de] |
| flood | **inondation** (f) | [inɔ̃dasjɔ̃] |

earthquake	**tremblement** (m) **de terre**	[trɑ̃bləmɑ̃ də tɛr]
tremor, quake	**secousse** (f)	[səkus]
epicenter	**épicentre** (m)	[episɑ̃tr]

| eruption | **éruption** (f) | [erypsjɔ̃] |
| lava | **lave** (f) | [lav] |

| tornado | **tornade** (f) | [tɔrnad] |
| typhoon | **typhon** (m) | [tifɔ̃] |

hurricane	**ouragan** (m)	[uragɑ̃]
storm	**tempête** (f)	[tɑ̃pɛt]
tsunami	**tsunami** (m)	[tsynami]

cyclone	**cyclone** (m)	[siklon]
bad weather	**intempéries** (f pl)	[ɛ̃tɑ̃peri]
fire (e.g., house on ~)	**incendie** (f)	[ɛ̃sɑ̃di]
disaster	**catastrophe** (f)	[katastrɔf]
meteorite	**météorite** (m)	[meteɔrit]

avalanche	**avalanche** (f)	[avalɑ̃ʃ]
snowslide	**éboulement** (m)	[ebulmɑ̃]
blizzard	**tempête** (f) **de neige**	[tɑ̃pɛt də nɛʒ]
snowstorm	**tempête** (f) **de neige**	[tɑ̃pɛt də nɛʒ]

FAUNA

87. Mammals. Predators

predator	**prédateur** (m)	[predatœr]
tiger	**tigre** (m)	[tigr]
lion	**lion** (m)	[ljɔ̃]
wolf	**loup** (m)	[lu]
fox	**renard** (m)	[rənar]
jaguar	**jaguar** (m)	[ʒagwar]
leopard	**léopard** (m)	[leɔpar]
cheetah	**guépard** (m)	[gepar]
black panther	**panthère** (f)	[pɑ̃tɛr]
puma	**puma** (m)	[pyma]
snow leopard	**léopard** (m) **de neiges**	[leɔpar də nɛʒ]
lynx	**lynx** (m)	[lɛ̃ks]
coyote	**coyote** (m)	[kɔjɔt]
jackal	**chacal** (m)	[ʃakal]
hyena	**hyène** (f)	[jɛn]

88. Wild animals

animal	**animal** (m)	[animal]
beast (animal)	**bête** (f)	[bɛt]
squirrel	**écureuil** (m)	[ekyrœj]
hedgehog	**hérisson** (m)	[erisɔ̃]
hare	**lièvre** (m)	[ljɛvr]
rabbit	**lapin** (m)	[lapɛ̃]
badger	**blaireau** (m)	[blɛro]
raccoon	**raton** (m)	[ratɔ̃]
hamster	**hamster** (m)	[amstɛr]
marmot	**marmotte** (f)	[marmɔt]
mole	**taupe** (f)	[top]
mouse	**souris** (f)	[suri]
rat	**rat** (m)	[ra]
bat	**chauve-souris** (f)	[ʃovsuri]
ermine	**hermine** (f)	[ɛrmin]
sable	**zibeline** (f)	[ziblin]

marten	**martre** (f)	[martr]
weasel	**belette** (f)	[bəlɛt]
mink	**vison** (m)	[vizõ]
beaver	**castor** (m)	[kastɔr]
otter	**loutre** (f)	[lutr]
horse	**cheval** (m)	[ʃəval]
moose	**élan** (m)	[elɑ̃]
deer	**cerf** (m)	[sɛr]
camel	**chameau** (m)	[ʃamo]
bison	**bison** (m)	[bizõ]
aurochs	**aurochs** (m)	[orɔk]
buffalo	**buffle** (m)	[byfl]
zebra	**zèbre** (m)	[zɛbr]
antelope	**antilope** (f)	[ɑ̃tilɔp]
roe deer	**chevreuil** (m)	[ʃəvrœj]
fallow deer	**biche** (f)	[biʃ]
chamois	**chamois** (m)	[ʃamwa]
wild boar	**sanglier** (m)	[sɑ̃glije]
whale	**baleine** (f)	[balɛn]
seal	**phoque** (m)	[fɔk]
walrus	**morse** (m)	[mɔrs]
fur seal	**otarie** (f)	[ɔtari]
dolphin	**dauphin** (m)	[dofɛ̃]
bear	**ours** (m)	[urs]
polar bear	**ours** (m) **blanc**	[urs blɑ̃]
panda	**panda** (m)	[pɑ̃da]
monkey	**singe** (m)	[sɛ̃ʒ]
chimpanzee	**chimpanzé** (m)	[ʃɛ̃pɑ̃ze]
orangutan	**orang-outang** (m)	[ɔrɑ̃utɑ̃]
gorilla	**gorille** (m)	[gɔrij]
macaque	**macaque** (m)	[makak]
gibbon	**gibbon** (m)	[ʒibõ]
elephant	**éléphant** (m)	[elefɑ̃]
rhinoceros	**rhinocéros** (m)	[rinɔserɔs]
giraffe	**girafe** (f)	[ʒiraf]
hippopotamus	**hippopotame** (m)	[ipɔpɔtam]
kangaroo	**kangourou** (m)	[kɑ̃guru]
koala (bear)	**koala** (m)	[kɔala]
mongoose	**mangouste** (f)	[mɑ̃gust]
chinchilla	**chinchilla** (m)	[ʃɛ̃ʃila]
skunk	**sconse** (m)	[skõs]
porcupine	**porc-épic** (m)	[pɔrkepik]

89. Domestic animals

cat	**chatte** (f)	[ʃat]
tomcat	**chat** (m)	[ʃa]
dog	**chien** (m)	[ʃjɛ̃]
horse	**cheval** (m)	[ʃəval]
stallion	**étalon** (m)	[etalɔ̃]
mare	**jument** (f)	[ʒymɑ̃]
cow	**vache** (f)	[vaʃ]
bull	**taureau** (m)	[tɔro]
ox	**bœuf** (m)	[bœf]
sheep	**brebis** (f)	[brəbi]
ram	**mouton** (m)	[mutɔ̃]
goat	**chèvre** (f)	[ʃɛvr]
billy goat, he-goat	**bouc** (m)	[buk]
donkey	**âne** (m)	[ɑn]
mule	**mulet** (m)	[mylɛ]
pig	**cochon** (m)	[kɔʃɔ̃]
piglet	**pourceau** (m)	[purso]
rabbit	**lapin** (m)	[lapɛ̃]
hen (chicken)	**poule** (f)	[pul]
rooster	**coq** (m)	[kɔk]
duck	**canard** (m)	[kanar]
drake	**canard** (m) **mâle**	[kanar mal]
goose	**oie** (f)	[wa]
turkey cock	**dindon** (m)	[dɛ̃dɔ̃]
turkey (hen)	**dinde** (f)	[dɛ̃d]
domestic animals	**animaux** (m pl) **domestiques**	[animo dɔmɛstik]
tame (e.g., ~ hamster)	**apprivoisé**	[aprivwaze]
to tame (vt)	**apprivoiser**	[aprivwaze]
to breed (vt)	**élever**	[elve]
farm	**ferme** (f)	[fɛrm]
poultry	**volaille** (f)	[vɔlaj]
cattle	**bétail** (m)	[betaj]
herd (of cattle, goats)	**troupeau** (m)	[trupo]
stable	**écurie** (f)	[ekyri]
pigpen	**porcherie** (f)	[pɔrʃəri]
cowshed	**vacherie** (f)	[vaʃri]
rabbit hutch	**cabane** (f) **à lapins**	[kaban ɑ lapɛ̃]
hen house	**poulailler** (m)	[pulaje]

90. Birds

bird	oiseau (m)	[wazo]
pigeon	pigeon (m)	[piʒɔ̃]
sparrow	moineau (m)	[mwano]
tit	mésange (f)	[mezɑ̃ʒ]
magpie	pie (f)	[pi]
raven	corbeau (m)	[kɔrbo]
hooded crow	corneille (f)	[kɔrnɛj]
jackdaw	choucas (m)	[ʃuka]
rook	freux (m)	[frø]
duck	canard (m)	[kanar]
goose	oie (f)	[wa]
pheasant	faisan (m)	[fəzɑ̃]
eagle	aigle (m)	[ɛgl]
hawk	épervier (m)	[epɛrvje]
falcon	faucon (m)	[fokɔ̃]
vulture	vautour (m)	[votur]
condor	condor (m)	[kɔ̃dɔr]
swan	cygne (m)	[siɲ]
crane	grue (f)	[gry]
stork	cigogne (f)	[sigɔɲ]
parrot	perroquet (m)	[perɔkɛ]
hummingbird	colibri (m)	[kɔlibri]
peacock	paon (m)	[pɑ̃]
ostrich	autruche (f)	[otryʃ]
heron	héron (m)	[erɔ̃]
flamingo	flamant (m)	[flamɑ̃]
pelican	pélican (m)	[pelikɑ̃]
nightingale	rossignol (m)	[rɔsiɲɔl]
swallow	hirondelle (f)	[irɔ̃dɛl]
fieldfare	merle (m)	[mɛrl]
song thrush	grive (f)	[griv]
blackbird	merle noir (m)	[mɛrl nwar]
swift	martinet (m)	[martinɛ]
lark	alouette (f)	[alwɛt]
quail	caille (f)	[kaj]
woodpecker	pivert (m)	[pivɛr]
cuckoo	coucou (m)	[kuku]
owl	chouette (f)	[ʃwɛt]
eagle owl	hibou (m)	[ibu]

wood grouse	tétras (m)	[tetra]
black grouse	tétras-lyre (m)	[tetralir]
partridge	perdrix (f)	[pɛrdri]
starling	étourneau (m)	[eturno]
canary	canari (m)	[kanari]
hazel grouse	gélinotte (f) des bois	[ʒelinɔt də bwa]
chaffinch	pinson (m)	[pɛ̃sɔ̃]
bullfinch	bouvreuil (m)	[buvrœj]
gull (seagull)	mouette (f)	[mwɛt]
albatross	albatros (m)	[albatros]
penguin	pingouin (m)	[pɛ̃gwɛ̃]

91. Fish. Marine animals

bream	brème (f)	[brɛm]
carp	carpe (f)	[karp]
perch	perche (f)	[pɛrʃ]
catfish	silure (m)	[silyr]
pike	brochet (m)	[brɔʃɛ]
salmon	saumon (m)	[somɔ̃]
sturgeon	esturgeon (m)	[ɛstyrʒɔ̃]
herring	hareng (m)	[arɑ̃]
Atlantic salmon	saumon (m)	[somɔ̃]
mackerel	maquereau (m)	[makro]
flatfish	flet (m)	[flɛ]
sander, pike perch	sandre (f)	[sɑ̃dr]
cod	morue (f)	[mɔry]
tuna	thon (m)	[tɔ̃]
trout	truite (f)	[trɥit]
eel	anguille (f)	[ɑ̃gij]
electric ray	torpille (f)	[tɔrpij]
moray eel	murène (f)	[myrɛn]
piranha	piranha (m)	[piraɲa]
shark	requin (m)	[rəkɛ̃]
dolphin	dauphin (m)	[dofɛ̃]
whale	baleine (f)	[balɛn]
crab	crabe (m)	[krab]
jellyfish	méduse (f)	[medyz]
octopus	pieuvre (f), poulpe (m)	[pjœvr], [pulp]
starfish	étoile (f) de mer	[etwal də mɛr]
sea urchin	oursin (m)	[ursɛ̃]

seahorse	**hippocampe** (m)	[ipɔkɑ̃p]
oyster	**huître** (f)	[ɥitr]
shrimp	**crevette** (f)	[krəvɛt]
lobster	**homard** (m)	[ɔmar]
spiny lobster	**langoustine** (f)	[lɑ̃gustin]

92. Amphibians. Reptiles

snake	**serpent** (m)	[sɛrpɑ̃]
poisonous	**venimeux**	[vənimø]
viper	**vipère** (f)	[vipɛr]
cobra	**cobra** (m)	[kɔbra]
python	**python** (m)	[pitɔ̃]
boa	**boa** (m)	[bɔa]
grass snake	**couleuvre** (f)	[kulœvr]
rattle snake	**serpent** (m) **à sonnettes**	[sɛrpɑ̃ ɑ sɔnɛt]
anaconda	**anaconda** (m)	[anakɔ̃da]
lizard	**lézard** (m)	[lezar]
iguana	**iguane** (m)	[igwan]
monitor lizard	**varan** (m)	[varɑ̃]
salamander	**salamandre** (f)	[salamɑ̃dr]
chameleon	**caméléon** (m)	[kameleɔ̃]
scorpion	**scorpion** (m)	[skɔrpjɔ̃]
turtle	**tortue** (f)	[tɔrty]
frog	**grenouille** (f)	[grənuj]
toad	**crapaud** (m)	[krapo]
crocodile	**crocodile** (m)	[krɔkɔdil]

93. Insects

insect, bug	**insecte** (m)	[ɛ̃sɛkt]
butterfly	**papillon** (m)	[papijɔ̃]
ant	**fourmi** (f)	[furmi]
fly	**mouche** (f)	[muʃ]
mosquito	**moustique** (m)	[mustik]
beetle	**scarabée** (m)	[skarabe]
wasp	**guêpe** (f)	[gɛp]
bee	**abeille** (f)	[abɛj]
bumblebee	**bourdon** (m)	[burdɔ̃]
gadfly	**syrphe** (m)	[sirf]
spider	**araignée** (f)	[areɲe]
spider's web	**toile** (f) **d'araignée**	[twal dareɲe]

dragonfly	**libellule** (f)	[libelyl]
grasshopper	**sauterelle** (f)	[sotrɛl]
moth (night butterfly)	**papillon** (m)	[papijɔ̃]
cockroach	**cafard** (m)	[kafar]
tick	**tique** (f)	[tik]
flea	**puce** (f)	[pys]
midge	**moucheron** (m)	[muʃrɔ̃]
locust	**criquet** (m)	[krikɛ]
snail	**escargot** (m)	[ɛskargo]
cricket	**grillon** (m)	[grijɔ̃]
lightning bug	**luciole** (f)	[lysjɔl]
ladybug	**coccinelle** (f)	[kɔksinɛl]
cockchafer	**hanneton** (m)	[antɔ̃]
leech	**sangsue** (f)	[sɑ̃sy]
caterpillar	**chenille** (f)	[ʃənij]
worm	**ver** (m)	[vɛr]
larva	**larve** (f)	[larv]

FLORA

94. Trees

tree	**arbre** (m)	[arbr]
deciduous	**à feuilles caduques**	[ɑ fœj kadyk]
coniferous	**conifère**	[kɔnifɛr]
evergreen	**sempervirent**	[sɛ̃pɛrvirɑ̃]
apple tree	**pommier** (m)	[pɔmje]
pear tree	**poirier** (m)	[pwarje]
cherry tree	**cerisier** (m)	[sərizje]
plum tree	**prunier** (m)	[prynje]
birch	**bouleau** (m)	[bulo]
oak	**chêne** (m)	[ʃɛn]
linden tree	**tilleul** (m)	[tijœl]
aspen	**tremble** (m)	[trɑ̃bl]
maple	**érable** (m)	[erabl]
fir tree	**sapin** (m)	[sapɛ̃]
pine	**pin** (m)	[pɛ̃]
larch	**mélèze** (m)	[melɛz]
silver fir	**épicéa** (m)	[episea]
cedar	**cèdre** (m)	[sɛdr]
poplar	**peuplier** (m)	[pøplije]
rowan	**sorbier** (m)	[sɔrbje]
willow	**saule** (m)	[sol]
alder	**aune** (m)	[on]
beech	**hêtre** (m)	[ɛtr]
elm	**orme** (m)	[ɔrm]
ash (tree)	**frêne** (m)	[frɛn]
chestnut	**marronnier** (m)	[marɔnje]
magnolia	**magnolia** (m)	[maɲɔlja]
palm tree	**palmier** (m)	[palmje]
cypress	**cyprès** (m)	[siprɛ]
mangrove	**palétuvier** (m)	[paletyvje]
baobab	**baobab** (m)	[baɔbab]
eucalyptus	**eucalyptus** (m)	[økaliptys]
redwood	**séquoia** (m)	[sekɔja]

95. Shrubs

bush	**buisson** (m)	[bɥisɔ̃]
shrub	**broussaille** (f)	[brusaj]
grapevine	**raisin** (m)	[rɛzɛ̃]
vineyard	**vigne** (f)	[viɲ]
raspberry bush	**framboise** (f)	[frãbwaz]
redcurrant bush	**groseille** (f) **rouge**	[grozɛj ruʒ]
gooseberry bush	**groseille** (f) **verte**	[grozɛj vɛrt]
acacia	**acacia** (m)	[akasja]
barberry	**berbéris** (m)	[bɛrberis]
jasmine	**jasmin** (m)	[ʒasmɛ̃]
juniper	**genévrier** (m)	[ʒənevrije]
rosebush	**rosier** (m)	[rozje]
dog rose	**églantier** (m)	[eglãtje]

96. Fruits. Berries

fruit	**fruit** (m)	[frɥi]
fruits	**fruits** (m pl)	[frɥi]
apple	**pomme** (f)	[pɔm]
pear	**poire** (f)	[pwar]
plum	**prune** (f)	[pryn]
strawberry	**fraise** (f)	[frɛz]
cherry	**cerise** (f)	[səriz]
grapes	**raisin** (m)	[rɛzɛ̃]
raspberry	**framboise** (f)	[frãbwaz]
blackcurrant	**cassis** (m)	[kasis]
redcurrant	**groseille** (f) **rouge**	[grozɛj ruʒ]
gooseberry	**groseille** (f) **verte**	[grozɛj vɛrt]
cranberry	**airelle** (f) **des marais**	[ɛrɛl de marɛ]
orange	**orange** (f)	[ɔrãʒ]
mandarin	**mandarine** (f)	[mãdarin]
pineapple	**ananas** (m)	[anana]
banana	**banane** (f)	[banan]
date	**datte** (f)	[dat]
lemon	**citron** (m)	[sitrɔ̃]
apricot	**abricot** (m)	[abriko]
peach	**pêche** (f)	[pɛʃ]
kiwi	**kiwi** (m)	[kiwi]

grapefruit	**pamplemousse** (m)	[pɑ̃pləmus]
berry	**baie** (f)	[bɛ]
berries	**baies** (f pl)	[bɛ]
cowberry	**airelle** (f) **rouge**	[ɛrɛl ruʒ]
field strawberry	**fraise** (f) **des bois**	[frɛz de bwa]
bilberry	**myrtille** (f)	[mirtij]

97. Flowers. Plants

flower	**fleur** (f)	[flœr]
bouquet (of flowers)	**bouquet** (m)	[bukɛ]
rose (flower)	**rose** (f)	[roz]
tulip	**tulipe** (f)	[tylip]
carnation	**oeillet** (m)	[œjɛ]
gladiolus	**glaïeul** (m)	[glajœl]
cornflower	**bleuet** (m)	[bløɛ]
bluebell	**campanule** (f)	[kɑ̃panyl]
dandelion	**dent-de-lion** (f)	[dɑ̃dəljɔ̃]
camomile	**marguerite** (f)	[margərit]
aloe	**aloès** (m)	[alɔɛs]
cactus	**cactus** (m)	[kaktys]
rubber plant	**ficus** (m)	[fikys]
lily	**lis** (m)	[li]
geranium	**géranium** (m)	[ʒeranjɔm]
hyacinth	**jacinthe** (f)	[ʒasɛ̃t]
mimosa	**mimosa** (m)	[mimɔza]
narcissus	**jonquille** (f)	[ʒɔ̃kij]
nasturtium	**capucine** (f)	[kapysin]
orchid	**orchidée** (f)	[ɔrkide]
peony	**pivoine** (f)	[pivwan]
violet	**violette** (f)	[vjɔlɛt]
pansy	**pensée** (f)	[pɑ̃se]
forget-me-not	**myosotis** (m)	[mjɔzɔtis]
daisy	**pâquerette** (f)	[pɑkrɛt]
poppy	**coquelicot** (m)	[kɔkliko]
hemp	**chanvre** (m)	[ʃɑ̃vr]
mint	**menthe** (f)	[mɑ̃t]
lily of the valley	**muguet** (m)	[mygɛ]
snowdrop	**perce-neige** (f)	[pɛrsənɛʒ]
nettle	**ortie** (f)	[ɔrti]
sorrel	**oseille** (f)	[ozɛj]

water lily	**nénuphar** (m)	[nenyfar]
fern	**fougère** (f)	[fuʒɛr]
lichen	**lichen** (m)	[likɛn]

greenhouse (tropical ~)	**serre** (f)	[sɛr]
lawn	**gazon** (m)	[gazõ]
flowerbed	**parterre** (m)	[partɛr]

plant	**plante** (f)	[plãt]
grass	**herbe** (f)	[ɛrb]
blade (of grass)	**brin** (m) **d'herbe**	[brɛ̃ dɛrb]

leaf	**feuille** (f)	[fœj]
petal (of flower)	**pétale** (f)	[petal]
stem (of plant)	**tige** (f)	[tiʒ]
tuber	**tubercule** (m)	[tybɛrkyl]

| young plant | **pousse** (f) | [pus] |
| thorn | **épine** (f) | [epin] |

to blossom (vi)	**fleurir**	[flœrir]
to fade, to wither	**se faner**	[sə fane]
smell (odor)	**odeur** (f)	[ɔdœr]
to cut (vt)	**couper**	[kupe]
to pick (a flower)	**cueillir**	[kœjir]

98. Cereals, grains

grain	**grains** (m pl)	[grɛ̃]
cereals	**céréales** (f pl)	[sereal]
ear (of grain)	**épi** (m)	[epi]

wheat	**blé** (m)	[ble]
rye	**seigle** (m)	[sɛgl]
oats	**avoine** (f)	[avwan]
millet	**millet** (m)	[mijɛ]
barley	**orge** (f)	[ɔrʒ]

corn	**maïs** (m)	[mais]
rice	**riz** (m)	[ri]
buckwheat	**sarrasin** (m)	[sarazɛ̃]

pea	**pois** (m)	[pwa]
kidney beans	**haricot** (m)	[ariko]
soy beans	**soja** (m)	[sɔʒa]
lentil	**lentille** (f)	[lãtij]

COUNTRIES OF THE WORLD

99. Countries. Part 1

Afghanistan	**Afghanistan** (m)	[afganistã]
Albania	**Albanie** (f)	[albani]
Argentina	**Argentine** (f)	[arʒãtin]
Armenia	**Arménie** (f)	[armeni]
Australia	**Australie** (f)	[ostrali]
Austria	**Autriche** (f)	[otriʃ]
Azerbaijan	**Azerbaïdjan** (m)	[azɛrbajdʒã]
Bahamas	**Bahamas** (f pl)	[baamas]
Bangladesh	**Bangladesh** (m)	[bãgladɛʃ]
Belarus	**Biélorussie** (f)	[bjelɔrysi]
Belgium	**Belgique** (f)	[bɛlʒik]
Bolivia	**Bolivie** (f)	[bɔlivi]
Bosnia-Herzegovina	**Bosnie** (f)	[bɔsni]
Brazil	**Brésil** (m)	[brezil]
Bulgaria	**Bulgarie** (f)	[bylgari]
Cambodia	**Cambodge** (m)	[kãbɔdʒ]
Canada	**Canada** (m)	[kanada]
Chile	**Chili** (m)	[ʃili]
China	**Chine** (f)	[ʃin]
Colombia	**Colombie** (f)	[kɔlõbi]
Croatia	**Croatie** (f)	[krɔasi]
Cuba	**Cuba** (f)	[kyba]
Cyprus	**Chypre** (m)	[ʃipr]
Denmark	**Danemark** (m)	[danmark]
Dominican Republic	**République** (f) **Dominicaine**	[repyblik dɔminikɛn]
Ecuador	**Équateur** (m)	[ekwatœr]
Egypt	**Égypte** (f)	[eʒipt]
England	**Angleterre** (f)	[ãglətɛr]
Estonia	**Estonie** (f)	[ɛstɔni]
Finland	**Finlande** (f)	[fɛlãd]
France	**France** (f)	[frãs]
French Polynesia	**Polynésie** (f) **Française**	[pɔlinezi frãsɛz]
Georgia	**Géorgie** (f)	[ʒeɔrʒi]
Germany	**Allemagne** (f)	[almaɲ]
Ghana	**Ghana** (m)	[gana]
Great Britain	**Grande-Bretagne** (f)	[grãdbrətaɲ]
Greece	**Grèce** (f)	[grɛs]

| Haiti | **Haïti** (m) | [aiti] |
| Hungary | **Hongrie** (f) | [ɔ̃gri] |

100. Countries. Part 2

Iceland	**Islande** (f)	[islãd]
India	**Inde** (f)	[ɛ̃d]
Indonesia	**Indonésie** (f)	[ɛ̃dɔnezi]
Iran	**Iran** (m)	[irã]
Iraq	**Iraq** (m)	[irak]
Ireland	**Irlande** (f)	[irlãd]
Israel	**Israël** (m)	[israɛl]
Italy	**Italie** (f)	[itali]

Jamaica	**Jamaïque** (f)	[ʒamaik]
Japan	**Japon** (m)	[ʒapɔ̃]
Jordan	**Jordanie** (f)	[ʒɔrdani]
Kazakhstan	**Kazakhstan** (m)	[kazakstã]
Kenya	**Kenya** (m)	[kenja]
Kirghizia	**Kirghizistan** (m)	[kirgizistã]
Korea	**Corée** (f)	[kɔre]
Kuwait	**Koweït** (m)	[kɔwɛjt]

Laos	**Laos** (m)	[laos]
Latvia	**Lettonie** (f)	[lɛtɔni]
Lebanon	**Liban** (m)	[libã]
Libya	**Libye** (f)	[libi]
Liechtenstein	**Liechtenstein** (m)	[liʃtɛnʃtajn]
Lithuania	**Lituanie** (f)	[lituani]
Luxembourg	**Luxembourg** (m)	[lyksãbur]

Macedonia	**Macédoine** (f)	[masedwan]
Madagascar	**Madagascar** (f)	[madagaskar]
Malaysia	**Malaisie** (f)	[malɛzi]
Malta	**Malte** (f)	[malt]
Mexico	**Mexique** (m)	[mɛksik]
Moldavia	**Moldavie** (f)	[mɔldavi]

Monaco	**Monaco** (m)	[mɔnako]
Mongolia	**Mongolie** (f)	[mɔ̃gɔli]
Montenegro	**Monténégro** (m)	[mɔ̃tenegro]
Morocco	**Maroc** (m)	[marɔk]
Myanmar	**Myanmar** (m)	[mjanmar]

Namibia	**Namibie** (f)	[namibi]
Nepal	**Népal** (m)	[nepal]
Netherlands	**Pays-Bas** (m)	[peiba]
New Zealand	**Nouvelle Zélande** (f)	[nuvɛl zelãd]
North Korea	**Corée** (f) **du Nord**	[kɔre dy nɔr]
Norway	**Norvège** (f)	[nɔrvɛʒ]

101. Countries. Part 3

Pakistan	**Pakistan** (m)	[pakistã]
Palestine	**Palestine** (f)	[palɛstin]
Panama	**Panamá** (m)	[panama]
Paraguay	**Paraguay** (m)	[paragwɛ]
Peru	**Pérou** (m)	[peru]
Poland	**Pologne** (f)	[pɔlɔɲ]
Portugal	**Portugal** (m)	[pɔrtygal]
Romania	**Roumanie** (f)	[rumani]
Russia	**Russie** (f)	[rysi]
Saudi Arabia	**Arabie** (f) **Saoudite**	[arabi saudit]
Scotland	**Écosse** (f)	[ekɔs]
Senegal	**Sénégal** (m)	[senegal]
Serbia	**Serbie** (f)	[sɛrbi]
Slovakia	**Slovaquie** (f)	[slɔvaki]
Slovenia	**Slovénie** (f)	[slɔveni]
South Africa	**République** (f) **Sud-africaine**	[repyblik sydafrikɛn]
South Korea	**Corée** (f) **du Sud**	[kɔre dy syd]
Spain	**Espagne** (f)	[ɛspaɲ]
Surinam	**Surinam** (m)	[syrinam]
Sweden	**Suède** (f)	[sɥɛd]
Switzerland	**Suisse** (f)	[sɥis]
Syria	**Syrie** (f)	[siri]
Taiwan	**Taïwan** (m)	[tajwan]
Tajikistan	**Tadjikistan** (m)	[tadʒikistã]
Tanzania	**Tanzanie** (f)	[tãzani]
Tasmania	**Tasmanie** (f)	[tasmani]
Thailand	**Thaïlande** (f)	[tajlãd]
The Czech Republic	**République** (f) **Tchèque**	[repyblik tʃɛk]
Tunisia	**Tunisie** (f)	[tynizi]
Turkey	**Turquie** (f)	[tyrki]
Turkmenistan	**Turkménistan** (m)	[tyrkmenistã]
Ukraine	**Ukraine** (f)	[ykrɛn]
United Arab Emirates	**Fédération** (f) **des Émirats Arabes Unis**	[federasjɔ̃ dezemira arabzyni]
United States of America	**les États Unis**	[lezeta zyni]
Uruguay	**Uruguay** (m)	[yrygwɛ]
Uzbekistan	**Ouzbékistan** (m)	[uzbekistã]
Vatican	**Vatican** (m)	[vatikã]
Venezuela	**Venezuela** (f)	[venezɥela]
Vietnam	**Vietnam** (m)	[vjɛtnam]
Zanzibar	**Zanzibar** (m)	[zãzibar]

2383400R00059

Printed in Great Britain
by Amazon.co.uk, Ltd.,
Marston Gate.